THE
QUIZ-SETTER'S
QUIZ BOOK

D0332833

Also available from Elliot Right Way Books

The Quizmaster's Quiz Book
Ready-Made Quizzes
Quirky Quiz Questions
How To Win Quizzes
How To Run A Quiz
How To Solve Cryptic Crosswords

Where to find *Right Way*

Elliot *Right Way* take pride in our editorial quality, accuracy and value-for-money. Booksellers everywhere can rapidly obtain any *Right Way* book for you. If you have been particularly pleased with any one title, do please mention this to your bookseller as personal recommendation helps us enormously.

Please send to the address on the back of the title page opposite, a stamped, self-addressed envelope if you would like a copy of our *free catalogue*. Alternatively, you may wish to browse through our extensive range of informative titles arranged by subject on the Internet at **www.right-way.co.uk**

We welcome views and suggestions from readers as well as from prospective authors; do please write to us or e-mail: **info@right-way.co.uk**

THE QUIZ-SETTER'S QUIZ BOOK

Don Wilson

RIGHT WAY

Copyright notice

© Elliot Right Way Books MCMXCVI

All rights reserved. No part of this book may be reproduced, stored in a retrieval system, or transmitted, in any form or by any means, electronic, photocopying, mechanical, recording or otherwise, without the prior permission of the copyright owner.

Conditions of sale
This book shall only be sold, lent, or hired, for profit, trade, or otherwise, in its original binding, except where special permission has been granted by the Publishers.

Whilst care is taken in selecting Authors who are authoritative in their subjects, it is emphasised that their books can reflect their knowledge only up to the time of writing. Information can be superseded and printers' errors can creep in. This book is sold, therefore, on the condition that neither Publisher nor Author can be held legally responsible for the consequences of any error or omission there may be.

Typeset in 11/13pt Times by Letterpart Ltd., Reigate, Surrey.

Printed and bound in Great Britain by Cox & Wyman Ltd., Reading, Berkshire.

The *Right Way* series is published by Elliot Right Way Books, Brighton Road, Lower Kingswood, Tadworth, Surrey, KT20 6TD, U.K. For more information about our company and the other books we publish visit our web site at www.right-way.co.uk

CONTENTS

DEDICATION

To my wife and family,
who keep asking me awkward questions.

INTRODUCTION

One of the problems of setting quizzes on a regular basis is that eventually the time comes when you find yourself pushed to find some questions to make up the quota. If, like all good quiz-setters, you prefer to devise your own questions, you just may not have the time to carry out the research necessary to produce brand new questions.

That's where this book comes into its own.

All quiz-setters are guilty at some time or other of dipping into books of quiz questions to supplement the weekly questions, and problems arise when you accept as correct the answers that appear in quiz books. I've had this happen to me a couple of times in the past, and now I accept nothing as fact unless I've seen the answer in a reference book. All the questions in this book have been verified and you can rely on them one hundred percent – I hope! If you do find an answer that is incorrect, award yourself a point!

I have also arranged the quiz rounds in this book in a different fashion. Often books contain the questions with the answers at the back of the book; others have the questions on one page and the answers on the next page. In either event you have to keep flipping backwards and forwards to check the answers to the questions. In this book the answer appears on the same page as the question so that you could – if you wished – ask the questions straight from the book and have the answer immediately in front of you should there be any queries. (This book could then be a real boon to you on that occasional night when you just haven't had time during the week to prepare questions for a particular night.)

Another problem with many quiz books is what I call 'the old chestnuts'. Some questions appear or are heard again and again so that there are times when contestants are writing the answers down before you have finished asking the questions! Hopefully you will find the vast majority of questions in this book fresh and interesting, but generally there will be a couple of 'easy' questions or 'chestnuts' in each round, if only to encourage the participants.

I go to quizzes regularly and believed for many years that there were only two types of question – those you could answer and those you could not answer – but I have mellowed somewhat over the years and believe there is a third type of question: those to which you can make an 'educated' guess. An example of this would be a question like: "Which metal is the main constituent of Britannia metal?" I'd never heard of Britannia metal, but I did know that in ancient times Britain was renowned for its tin mines so an 'educated' guess came up trumps. "Which jacket took its name from the club in New York where it was introduced?" The answer was hardly likely to be a Norfolk Jacket, but "club" suggested something special and 'Tuxedo' would be – and was – a good guess.

You will find some regular threads running through the questions, and I'd like to say a few words about these. You will find the pop music questions to be rather 'bald' ones because the pop music scene is so fast moving that these questions will always last. You will find that there are a lot of 'choice' answers. Some people aren't sold on questions where those taking part are given a choice of answers, but I feel that by offering a choice it gives everyone taking part a reasonable chance of coming up with the correct answer, and the more astute competitors can generally work out which answer will give them the point. If you, as question-setter, wish to omit the choices and simply ask the question and leave it at that, well, that's entirely up to you. Finally you will find 'True or False' statements crop up occasionally. I always find when taking part in quizzes that 'questions' like this can cause a great deal of thought and effort and so I've included a good selection of these.

The main part of the book comprises 100 Rounds of 'straightforward' quizzes. Then there is a small selection of 'Thematic' quizzes which were once very popular in the area in which I live. Even if you don't use them, they might give you some ideas when setting your own quizzes. At the end of the book you will find some pages of 'Tie Breaker' questions for those occasions when you want a winner or a second or third. These are really questions which by and large you don't expect people to answer correctly, but you will obtain the winner you need because someone will be the closest to the answer. You could also use them for your accumulative Jackpot or Snowball each week if you have one, or for a weekly one-off question when for an extra payment contestants can have a guess at one question, winner take all. If there is no winner, the money rolls over to the next week. I use a book of raffle tickets for this – participants write their answer on one half of each paired ticket and hand it in. You then check the answers and if you have a winner it's an easy matter to announce who has won. This always goes down well at the quiz I currently run.

I hope you find this book useful and continue to have many pleasant evenings as quiz-setter.

And good luck to Ken Eastpoint and Oswald Lindon!

Don Wilson

ROUNDS

Round 1

1. What colour is traditionally associated with Roman emperors? **Purple**

2. What name is given to the flap of cartilage which prevents food from entering your windpipe? **Epiglottis**

3. What sort of fruit is a Laxton Superb? Is it an apple, a strawberry or a plum? **Apple**

4. Under what name did Lord Tweedsmuir write several novels? **John Buchan**

5. What is the more common name for grape-sugar? Is it gluten, glucose or lactose? **Glucose**

6. What is a labret? Is it the front part of an insect's head, an ornament inserted through the lip, or culpable negligence in legal matters? **A lip ornament**

7. Areas of equal . . . . . . (what) are connected by a line called an isohyet on a map? **Rainfall**

8. In which American state are the towns of Anaconda and Moscow and the Salmon River? **Idaho**

9. In which sport is there competition for the America's Cup? **Yachting**

10. Which British island, about 80 feet across, is in the Atlantic, 230 miles west of the Hebrides?   **Rockall**

11. What was supposed to flow in the veins of the Greek gods?   **Ichor**

12. In which film did POWs use a vaulting horse to disguise the digging of an escape tunnel?   ***The Wooden Horse***

13. Which drink was advertised by Leonard Rossiter and Joan Collins?   **Cinzano**

14. What was the name of the aging rock band in the 1987 TV series *Tutti Frutti*?   **The Majestics**

15. Which straits separate Sri Lanka from India? Is it the Straits of Jaffna, the Comorin Straits or the Palk Straits?   **The Palk Straits**

16. True or false: Glyndebourne Opera House is in East Sussex?   **True**

17. Who designed the tapestry which hangs behind the altar in Coventry Cathedral?   **Graham Sutherland**

18. Which animal gives us nutria fur? Is it the capybara, coypu or wolverine?   **Coypu**

19. Who said: "It's a funny old world – a man's lucky if he gets out of it alive."?   **W C Fields**

20. What is the collective word for a group of foxes?   **Skulk**

Round 2

1. In which novel did Michael Henchard sell his wife for 5 guineas?   ***The Mayor of Casterbridge***

2. For which English king did Handel compose his
    Water Music?   **George I**

3. What colour was Alexandre Dumas' tulip?   **Black**

4. What is the square root of 729?   **27**

5. On what material does a topiarist work?   **Hedges
                                                  and shrubs**

6. In which club did Arthur and Terry drink in the TV
    series *Minder*?   **The Winchester**

7. Which famous adventure story was originally titled
    The Sea Cook?   *Treasure Island*

8. Mainly which creatures belong to the order
    arachnida?   **Spiders**

9. From which country did the Bashi Bazouks come?
    Was it Turkey, Morocco or Persia?   **Turkey**

10. Which fruit did Columbus discover on Guadeloupe
    in 1493? Was it the pineapple, banana or the melon?
                                                Pineapple

11. Who played the named character in these films?
    Darby's Rangers, *Mister Buddwing* and *Marlowe*?
                                              James Garner

12. True or false: there is actually a country named
    Cape Verde?   **True**

13. Which Christian name derives from the Gaelic for
    'handsome'?   **Kenneth**

14. From what affliction did the patient Job suffer in
    the Bible? Was it leprosy, boils or blindness?   **Boils**

15. What is the family name of the Dukes of
    Wellington?   **Wellesley**

16.   In which city were the 1896 Olympic Games held?
                                                Athens

17.   What is the sport for which Sabina Park is famous?
                                                Cricket

18.   In *Macbeth*, who was Banquo's son? Was it
      Fleance, Donalbain or Seyton?   **Fleance**

19.   Who had a hit in 1972 with *Sylvia's Mother*?
                                            Doctor Hook

20.   Which English football club play at Roots Hall?
                                        Southend United

Round 3

1.   In which film did Lee Marvin throw boiling coffee
      in Gloria Grahame's face?   ***The Big Heat***

2.   Which gas is manufactured by the Haber Process?
      Is it ammonia, chlorine or helium?   **Ammonia**

3.   Who owned the High Chaparral ranch?   **John
                                                Cannon**

4.   Two musical notes have no actual flats. Name one.
                                                C or F

5.   If a woman is nubile, what does that mean?
                                            Marrigeable

6.   What is an odalisque? Is it a room in a mosque, a
      female slave or a stone in Stonehenge?   **Female
                                                slave**

7.   What does a mycologist study? Is it mosses, fungi or
      muscles?   **Fungi**

8.   True or false: Henry Patrick McCarty was Billy the Kid's real name?   **True**

9.   Who said: "The great masses of the people will more easily fall victim to a big lie than to a small one."?   **Hitler**

10.   Who had Top Ten hits in the 1980s with *Run To the Hills*, *Can I Play With Madness* and *The Evil That Men Do*?   **Iron Maiden**

11.   Who sailed away to die on HMS *Bellerophon*?
                                                    Napoleon

12.   What was the actual practical purpose of a gargoyle?   **Water spout**

13.   What finally stood in for Roy Hattersley when he couldn't appear on *Have I Got News For You* on TV?   **A tub of lard**

14.   What were once called 'love apples'?   **Tomatoes**

15.   What is tilth? Is it cultivation, a type of rock, or a mark placed over 'n' in some Spanish words?
                                                    Cultivation

16.   What originally gave foolscap paper its name?
                                                    The watermark

17.   In which sport is there something named after Ulrich Salchow?   **Ice Skating**

18.   In a famous Dickens novel, who was helped financially by Abel Magwitch?   **Pip**

19.   After which famous engineer is the university at Uxbridge named?   **Brunel**

20.   If ursine is bearlike and equine horselike, what is vulpine?   **Foxlike**

Round 4

1. Devil's apron and purple laver are types of what?
   Seaweed

2. Who was the father of David? Was it Zachariah, Absalom or Jesse?
   Jesse

3. Under what nickname did Albert de Salvo become infamous?
   The Boston Strangler

4. True or false: vernal means easily bribed?   **False**
   (It means to do with spring.)

5. What is the name of the metal discs in the rim of a tambourine? Are they pings, tinklers or jingles?
   Jingles

6. In Gaelic legend, who had a dog called Bran?
   Fingal

7. Who played Eliza Doolittle in the film *My Fair Lady*?
   Audrey Hepburn

8. What are ossicles and osselets?   **Bones**

9. Soling, Star and Finn are categories in which sport?
   Yachting

10. Which device allows a car's driving wheels to turn at different speeds when cornering?   **Differential**

11. Which large object was discovered by Clyde Tombaugh in 1930?
    Pluto

12. Disc jockey Alan Freed popularised and helped to name which type of music from 1951?   **Rock 'n Roll**

13. In poker, which is the best hand of flush, run (straight) and three of a kind?
    Flush

14. Which King of England's mother and son were
    both beheaded?   **James I's**

15. To what is the French word 'chambré' applied?
                                              Wine

16. True or false: Dashiel Hammett created the
    detective Philip Marlowe?   **False**
                        (Raymond Chandler did.)

17. To what does the adjective 'Pontic' apply?   **The**
                                          Black Sea

18. What term is used to measure the fineness of yarns?
                                            Denier

19. Is charlock a herb, a disease or a moth?   **A herb**

20. What is the 2nd of February called in the USA?
                                     Ground-hog Day

Round 5

1. What does the abbreviation GDP stand for?
                           Gross Domestic Product

2. Who played the named character in these films?
   Kitty Foyle, *Roxie Hart* and *Magnificent Doll*?
                                      Ginger Rogers

3. Which calendar did Britain adopt in 1752?
                                         Gregorian

4. Who presented the TV show *Sweethearts* in 1987?
                                      Larry Grayson

5. After which Norse goddess is Friday named?
                                    Frigga or Freya

6.   In 1993, which country ranked 3rd in terms of population? Was it India, USA or Indonesia?

USA

7.   Which of the Seven Wonders of the World was constructed by the sculptor Phidias about 430 BC?

Statue of Zeus

8.   Who is the patron saint of singers? Is it Gregory, Vitus or Andrew?   **St Gregory**

9.   Which video-cassette system, introduced in the 1970s, couldn't compete with VHS and disappeared?   **Betamax**

10. What is the Greek equivalent of the Roman deity Pax?   **Irene**

11. Who had a No 1 with *Reet Petite* almost 30 years after he first had it in the Top Ten?   **Jackie Wilson**

12. True or false: the Egyptian god Osiris was the son of Nut?   **True**

13. Of which country was Achmed Sukarno President from 1945 to 1962?   **Indonesia**

14. Which German physicist formulated the quantum theory?   **Max Planck**

15. What is pott? Is it a paper size, re-fired pottery or a consultation?   **Paper size**

16. In what field did Norman Parkinson make his name?   **Photography**

17. What instrument was played by jazz musician John Coltrane?   **Saxophone**

18. Which novel by Michael Crichton was No 1 bestseller paperback in 1993?   *Jurassic Park*

19. In which sport did Irina Rodnina win 23 World, Olympic and European gold medals?   **Ice skating**

20. Who won Best Actress Oscar for her role in *Coming Home* (1978)?   **Jane Fonda**

Round 6

1. From whom did Shylock wish to take his pound of flesh?   **Antonio**

2. Who wrote the plays *Arms and the Man* and *The Devil's Disciple*?   **G B Shaw**

3. The Jewish festival Purim celebrates the story of which woman in the Bible?   **Esther**

4. What colour eggs are the Chinese symbol of luck and new life?   **Red**

5. In the Bible which king's doom was foretold by the writing on the wall?   **Belshazzar**

6. Which once common disease was also known as The White Death?   **Tuberculosis**

7. Spell Humorous.   **Humorous**

8. True or false: Salisbury Crags are in Edinburgh?   **True**

9. In which African country do the Hausa people live?   **Nigeria**

10. Who succeeded U Thant as Secretary General of the UN?   **Kurt Waldheim**

11. Which bone is between your femur and your tibia?   **Patella**

12. Under what name did Nathan Birnbaum become famous? **George Burns**

13. Of what do fennel leaves taste? Is it onion, pepper or aniseed? **Aniseed**

14. Who was Desmond Lynam's co-presenter on the first series of *How Do They Do That*? **Jennie Hull**

15. Which French soldier's name became the word for a strict disciplinarian? **(Jean) Martinet**

16. How many islands make up the Maldives? Is it (roughly) 850, 1200 or 1500? **1200 (1196)**

17. Which film ends like this? Mounted Soldier (Charlton Heston) reaches out to a little girl and says: "Here, take my hand"? **55 Days at Peking**

18. Which singer had Top Ten hits in the 1980s with *Games Without Frontiers* and *Sledgehammer*? **Peter Gabriel**

19. In which constellation is the star Betelgeuse? **Orion**

20. Who was the Norse god of poetry? Was it Bragi, Balder or Hoder? **Bragi**

Round 7

1. How many players are there in a baseball team? **Nine**

2. What was the name of the Hoover Dam on the Colorado River from 1933 to 1947? **Boulder Dam**

3. How long is a Gunter's chain? Is it 66 feet, 100 feet or 144 feet? **66 feet**

4.   True or false: Athos, Porthos and Aramis all appear in the novel *Vicomte de Bragelonne*?   **True**

5.   What was to be suppressed by 'comstockery'?
Corrupting literature

6.   Russian, Fleury, Tau and Papal are all types of what?   **Crosses**

7.   Who said: "I'll bet your father spent the first year of your life throwing rocks at the stork."?   **Groucho Marx**

8.   Who was the guzzling and greedy giant created by Rabelais?   **Gargantua**

9.   Which natural feature has been nicknamed The Lamp of Phoebus?   **The sun**

10. Which Quaker founded the city of Philadelphia?
William Penn

11. In which film, based on Conrad's *Heart of Darkness*, did Martin Sheen seek Marlon Brando?
Apocalypse Now

12. Who defined the Four Freedoms in 1941?
Franklin D Roosevelt

13. Which sport is now believed to be the origin of the expression 'The Real McCoy'?   **Boxing**

14. Which bird is nicknamed Pharaoh's Chicken?
(Egyptian) Vulture

15. Which vocal group comprised Cass, Michelle, John and Denny?   **The Mamas and The Papas**

16. Which helpful organisation was founded by the Rev Chad Varah in 1953?   **Samaritans**

17. What name was and is used by American Black Nationalists for negroes who are too subservient to white people? **Uncle Tom**

18. What was the name of the cook in TV's *Upstairs Downstairs*? **Mrs Bridges**

19. Whom does Viola love in *Twelfth Night*? **Duke Orsino**

20. True or false: saxifrage is a small rock plant? **True**

Round 8

1. Who originally travelled the Via Dolorosa? **Jesus**

2. In the RAF how many squadrons make up a wing? **Three**

3. Which part of Britain, because of local pronunciation, is sometimes called Zedland? **The West Country**

4. What instrument is played by the leader of an orchestra? **Violin**

5. Who produced an album called *An Innocent Man*? **Billy Joel**

6. Which Archbishop of Canterbury, later canonised, was said to have seized the devil's nose in a pair of red-hot tongs? **Dunstan**

7. In the nursery rhyme, who visited the person with a little nut tree? **The King of Spain's daughter**

8. Who said: "The maxim of the British people is 'Business as usual'."? **Winston Churchill**

9.   What is a grackle? Is it a fish, a lizard or a bird?
Bird (Oriole)

10. Add together Buchan's steps, Sayers' Tailors and Rome's hills.
55 (39+9+7)

11. What was revealed by a letter to Lord Monteagle?
The Gunpowder Plot

12. In which TV series did Richard Chamberlain play an Australian priest whose son also became a priest?
The Thorn Birds

13. Which slang word for prison came into use from the name of a famous gaol in Southwark in London?
Clink

14. Which of these is NOT a member of the antelope family: impala, eland, hyrax, dik-dik?
Hyrax

15. What kind of cross-country running involves two runners setting off early and leaving a trail for the chasing runners to follow?
Hare and Hounds

16. True or false: the National Anthem of Portugal is *Our Fatherland*?
False
(Portugal's is *The Portuguese*.)

17. What is the name of the dinosaur monster which has appeared in many Japanese films?
Godzilla

18. In which religion is the mystic formula Om Mani Padme Hum chanted?
Buddhism

19. How much would you be paid if you held an honorary post?
Nothing

20. In ancient mythology, what was a lamia? A fabulous horse, a female demon or a magic shield?
Female demon

Round 9

1. In fairy folklore, what was the job of Mab?

   Midwife

2. In the Bible, what instrument did David play?

   Harp

3. In which British city was the the warning cry "Gardy Loo" used when people upstairs were emptying the slop out of the window?   **Edinburgh**

4. In the TV series *Edward and Mrs Simpson*, who played Edward?   **Edward Fox**

5. Which country has the motto "E Pluribus Unum" on its Great Seal?   **USA**

6. What was the title of the spoof version of *The Maltese Falcon*, made in 1975 and starring George Segal as Sam Spade Jr.?   ***The Black Bird***

7. Which literary character rode a horse called Rosinante?   **Don Quixote**

8. Under a now obselete system, who would be granted a Ticket of Leave?   **A convict**
   (A type of parole.)

9. What is Tiddy-oggie? Is it a Cornish pasty, a Welsh stew or a Norfolk fish pie?   **Cornish pasty**

10. Who had Top Ten hits in the 1960s with *Detroit City*, *I'm Coming Home* and *Love Me Tonight*?

    Tom Jones

11. How many players did England use in the 1966 Football World Cup Finals? Was it 15, 16 or 17?

12. In which Commonwealth country is Waitangi Day the national day? **New Zealand**

13. True or false: Zoroastrianism is an ancient Turkish religion? **False (Persian)**

14. Who played Michael Douglas's wife in *Fatal Attraction*? **Anne Archer**

15. What name is given to foolishly extravagant or useless structures built for amusement or pride? **Follies**

16. Which one word fits these definitions: a small falcon, a small horse and a pastime? **Hobby**

17. According to Revelations, what is the number of the Beast? **666**

18. On whose shoulders did the Old Man of the Sea hoist himself? **Sinbad the Sailor's**

19. Which Motor Racing team is named after India's sacred flower? **Lotus**

20. What are you seeking if you hold out an olive branch? **Peace**

Round 10

1. In Western frontier towns, what were the cemeteries usually called? **Boot Hill**

2. Boosening, immersing people in cold water, was an old method of treating what? Was it drunkenness, insanity or possession? **Insanity**

3. Which famous building was erected for the Great Exhibition of 1851? **Crystal Palace**

4. Which industry was launched by David McConnell in 1886 as a result of his selling volumes of Shakespeare door to door?   **Cosmetics**

5. Which English king's son was nicknamed Prince Titi?   **George II's**

6. Is a killick a stone used as an anchor, a murderous ruffian or a man's tunic?   **Stone anchor**

7. What are said to be pulled out of the fire when retrieving a difficult situation for somebody?
                                                    Chestnuts

8. Which saint was shot to death by arrows in 288 AD?   **Sebastian**

9. True or false: the Tolpuddle Martyrs formed a trade union in Wiltshire?   **False (It was in Dorset.)**

10. Who succeeded Robert the Bruce as King of the Scots?   **David II**

11. Who owned the factory visited by Charlie Bucket in a Roald Dahl story?   **Willie Wonka**

12. In which Essex town can a couple compete for a flitch as a prize for being happily married?
                                                      Dunmow

13. For which county did Godfrey Evans play cricket?
                                                          Kent

14. What was the name for the ancient trade route between China and the Mediterranean?   **Silk Road**

15. Where did Lord Kitchener defeat the Mahdi in 1898?   **Omdurman**

16. Which disease is tested for by the Schich Test?
                                                    Diphtheria

17. With what art form was Donald McGill
    particularly associated?   **Seaside postcards**

18. Who had Top Ten hits in the 1980s with *I'm Still
    Standing*, *Passengers* and *Blue Eyes*?   **Elton John**

19. In which L P Hartley novel does a boy carry
    messages between two lovers?   ***The Go-Between***

20. For what was amateur naturalist Thomas Bewick
    especially famous?   **Engravings**

Round 11

1. In which US State are the Sierra Nevada
   mountains?   **California**

2. Which island off the north coast of Devon takes its
   name from the Norse word for puffin?   **Lundy**

3. Who played the murderer in *Kind Hearts and
   Coronets*?   **Dennis Price**

4. Which word connects crab, mite, monkey, plant
   and wasp?   **Spider**

5. True or false: Panay is an island in the Philippines?
           True

6. On which London street is Selfridges?   **Oxford Sreet**

7. A strobilus is another name for a pine cone, an
   orchid stamen or a tulip bulb?   **Pine Cone**

8. Which World War 2 leader was executed and
   exhibited by his own people?   **Mussolini**

9. What name is given to stunted and withered apples
   used to make rough cider?   **Scrumps**

10. Shorthorn cattle were the first breed to have their own herdbook. In which county were they developed? **Durham**

11. Who was crop-dusted in the film *North By Northwest*? **Cary Grant**

12. In *Treasure Island*, who, apart from Jim Hawkins, narrates part of the story? **Dr Livesey**

13. Marcus Samuel developed Shell Oil, but what was the original family business? Was it importing tin, importing sea shells and curios, or dealing in spices? **Importing sea shells**

14. Which American became World Chess Champion in 1972? **Bobby Fischer**

15. Who wrote the drama series *The Singing Detective*? **Dennis Potter**

16. What was once the traditional name for the holiday period in northern industrial towns? **Wakes Week**

17. Which Dutch player became Wimbledon Champion in 1996? **Richard Krajicek**

18. Who built Wormwood Scrubs? **The convicts**
(Contractors built the first nine cells then the nine convicts built the next nine, and so on.)

19. Is gneiss a type of rock, a moss or a young salmon? **Rock**

20. What was Newcastle University called when it was a college of Durham University? **King's College**

Round 12

1. True or false: Amy Johnson was American?   **False (She was British.)**

2. Who led the Scottish forces at Bannockburn?
    Robert the Bruce

3. Who traded places with Eddie Murphy in *Trading Places*?   **Dan Akroyd**

4. Which part of Britain was called Vectis by the Romans?   **Isle of Wight**

5. Who narrated the 26 part TV series *The World at War*?   **Laurence Olivier**

6. Tarquin the Proud was the last king of where?
    Rome

7. Which country's largest and oldest city was partly developed by a convict called Francis Greenaway?
    Australia's (Sydney)

8. On which river are the Victoria Falls?   **Zambezi**

9. In Chinese cosmology, what is the contrast and complement to the Yin?   **The Yang**

10. Is a saxhorn a plant, a musical instrument or an antelope?   **Musical instrument**

11. Vinegar is a dilute solution of which acid?   **Acetic**

12. Who, in 1907, was the first woman to receive the Order of Merit?   **Florence Nightingale**

13. In which sport were Barry Briggs and Ove Fundin World Champions?   **Speedway**

14. Who had Top Ten hits in the 1970s with *Come On Over To My Place*, *There Goes My First Love* and *Kissin' In the Back Row of the Movies*?   **The Drifters**

15. Which idol did the Israelites make when they believed Moses would not return from Mount Sinai?   **The Golden Calf**

16. What does the Dewey Decimal System classify?
                                                (Library) Books

17. True or false: I Ching is a Chinese method of divination?   **True**

18. Which German scholar sold his soul to the devil in return for power and knowledge?   **Faust**

19. What is sorghum? Is it a herb, a mineral oxide or a cereal crop?   **Cereal crop**

20. What was Lester Piggott's first Derby winner?
                                                Never Say Die

Round 13

1. What did Colonel Thomas Blood attempt to steal in 1671?   **Crown Jewels**

2. Who wrote *Journey To the Centre of the Earth*?
                                                Jules Verne

3. Which capital city is heated by volcanic springs? Is it Reykjavik, Helsinki or Wellington?   **Reykjavik**

4. Whose only No 1 was *I'm Into Something Good*?
                                                Herman's Hermits

5. Which writer described the 1920s as The Jazz Age?
                                                F Scott Fitzgerald

6. Who said: "I used to be Snow White but I drifted."?
    Mae West

7. In a classic film, whom did film producer Carl Denham bring to New York and bill as "The Eighth Wonder of the World"?   **King Kong**

8. What substance did Lister use to improve the hygiene of surgical operations?   **Carbolic Acid**

9. On TV, who co-starred with Roger Moore in *The Persuaders*?   **Tony Curtis**

10. Which US playwright wrote *Barefoot in the Park* and *The Odd Couple*?   **Neil Simon**

11. In which US state is Little Rock, scene of race riots in 1957? Is it Arkansas, Alabama or South Carolina?   **Arkansas**

12. What is America's National Cemetery called?
    Arlington

13. True or false: Arnhem Land is in the Netherlands?
    False (It is in Australia.)

14. Who was Governor of the Bahamas during World War 2?   **Duke of Windsor**

15. Whom did New Zealand beat 145-17 in the 1995 Rugby Union World Cup?   **Japan**

16. After Windsor, which is the largest castle in Britain? Is it Warwick, Caerphilly or Stirling?   **Caerphilly**

17. The pop duo Annie Lennox and Dave Stewart recorded under what name?   **Eurythmics**

18. In which country was Salman Rushdie born? Was it Turkey, India or Malaya?   **India**

19. Of which bird did Wordsworth write: "While I am lying on the grass / Thy twofold shout I hear"?

The cuckoo

20. How did the killer mark his victims in *No Way To Treat a Lady*? **Lipstick kiss on brow**

Round 14

1. What was Commonwealth Day called before 1958?

Empire Day

2. What name is given to expressions like 'catch the town drain' and 'tasted two worms'? **Spoonerism**

3. What are the corns in corned beef? **Salt**

4. Who played the Queen in the 1991 TV play *A Question of Attribution*? **Prunella Scales**

5. Which character from a comic was known as The Pilot of the Future? **Dan Dare**

6. Who was World Darts Champion 5 times between 1980 and 1986? **Eric Bristow**

7. What kind of animal is a Wessex Saddleback? **Pig**

8. Mary O'Brien is the real name of Lulu, Sandie Shaw or Dusty Springfield? **Dusty Springfield**

9. True or false: Dorothea Brooke is the central character of *Middlemarch*? **True**

10. In which country is Encyclopaedia Britannica published? **USA**

11. If you were using English Bond or Flemish Bond what would you be doing? **Bricklaying**

12. In *Gulliver's Travels* what form did the Yahoos take?   **Human form**

13. Which chain of stores was founded by Selim Zilkha in 1961? Was it Mothercare, Next, or Argos?
                                          Mothercare

14. Whose early days, allegedly, were depicted in the film *Wish You Were Here*?   **Cynthia Payne's**

15. Robert Plant was lead singer with which group founded in 1968?   **Led Zeppelin**

16. What is the common name for a myocardial infarction?   **Heart attack**

17. Is loess a moss, a legal term or a kind of soil?   **Soil**

18. 'Run off you girls; boys in view' is a memory aid for what?   **The colours of the rainbow**

19. Who directed and starred in the film *Yentl*?
                                       Barbra Streisand

20. How many cubic centimetres are there in a cubic metre?   **One million**

Round 15

1. Which locomotive still holds the speed record for steam locomotives?   **The *Mallard***

2. Does a pedologist study soils, feet or schoolchildren?
                                               Soils

3. Which stretch of water separates Denmark from Sweden?   **The Kattegat**

4. What is your philtrum? Is it a bone in your ear, a valve in your heart or the groove between nose and top lip?   **The groove between nose and top lip**

5. True or false: a gribble is a sea creature?   **True (It is a crustacean.)**

6. What is the common name for the garden flower *Dianthus barbatus*?   **Sweet William**

7. Complete this Munich quartet: Chamberlain, Hitler, Mussolini and . . . . . .?   **Daladier**

8. Upon which town's streets was Monopoly originally based?   **Atlantic City's**

9. Which of these did NOT captain England at cricket: Lamb, Boycott or Snow?   **Snow**

10. At which battle of 1798 did the boy stand on the burning deck?   **Battle of the Nile**

11. For what kind of paintings was Alfred Munnings famous?   **Horses**

12. In legend, who was the last King of Troy?   **Priam**

13. Which University has a rowing eight called Isis?   **Oxford**

14. Mr Tupman, Mr Snodgrass and Mr Winkle were members of which club?   **The Pickwick Club**

15. Since 1969 who is the only man, apart from Stephen Hendry, to have won 4 successive World Snooker Championships?   **Ray Reardon**

16. Which actor thought he was the man who shot Liberty Valance?   **James Stewart**

17. Only two Americans have won the Formula 1 Motor Racing Championship. Name one. **Phil Hill or Mario Andretti**

18. What nationality was the traitor Vidkun Quisling? Was he Norwegian, Danish or Dutch? **Norwegian**

19. What is the collective name for beavers? **Colony**

20. In which town was the Spode pottery works established in the 1760s? Was it Stoke, Derby or Worcester? **Stoke**

Round 16

1. True or false: in the radio series the Dales lived in Ambridge? **False (They lived in Kenton and then Exton New Town.)**

2. Which Hindu sect strangled travellers and worshipped Kali? **Thugs**

3. Which country is the major exporter of teak? **Burma (Myanmar)**

4. Which Royal House ruled England from 1461 to 1485? Was it York, Tudor or Stuart? **York**

5. In which TV time travel series does Scott Bakula play the lead? ***Quantum Leap***

6. At which sport was Fred Perry World Champion in 1929? **Table Tennis**

7. Who wrote *The Magus*, *The French Lieutenant's Woman* and *Daniel Martin*? **John Fowles**

8. In Hebrew, does the name Satan mean angel, devil or adversary? **Adversary**

9. Who engaged in the old American custom of bundling? Was it cloth merchants, engaged couples or lawyers? **Engaged couples**

10. Which club won the Scottish FA Cup three times from 1982 to 1984? Was it Celtic, Rangers or Aberdeen? **Aberdeen**

11. Which children's writer, Mrs Heelis, spent 30 years breeding Herdwick sheep? **Beatrix Potter**

12. Of what was the Greek goddess Nyx the personification? **Night**

13. What is smut? Is it a plant disease, a food fish or a duck? **Plant disease**

14. In *Casablanca* who played Sam, the piano player? **Dooley Wilson**

15. Which city, now in West China, is the capital of Tibet? **Lhasa**

16. Which Saint's Feast Day is July 15th? Is it Bartholomew, Martin or Swithin? **Swithin**

17. True or false: the Cat and Mouse Act was used against the suffragettes? **True**

18. In Moscow, what is Tsar Kolokol? **(World's heaviest) Bell**

19. John Grey Gorton was Prime Minister of which country? **Australia**

20. Which Roman palace is one mile west of Chichester? **Fishbourne**

Round 17

1. Who was the first signatory of the American Declaration of Independence? **John Hancock**

2. True or false: a 'Cheater' was originally a tax-collector? **True (from Escheator, an officer of the Exchequer)**

3. Who painted the ceiling of the Sistine Chapel? **Michelangelo**

4. Chaka, Dingaan and Cetewayo were leaders of which people? **Zulus**

5. Who wrote *Tropic of Cancer* and *Tropic of Capricorn*? **Henry Miller**

6. In what country is the Algarve? **Portugal**

7. In which film did Bob Hoskins play a black prostitute's minder? ***Mona Lisa***

8. Who, in 1941, designed and made the first viable helicopter? **Sikorsky**

9. Does a table tennis ball weigh between 34/36gms, 37/39gms or 38/40gms? **37/39gms**

10. In what country is the port of Archangel? **Russia**

11. What was the setting for the 1984 TV series *Tripper's Day*? **Supermarket**

12. Does 'gravid' mean serious, engraved or pregnant? **Pregnant**

13. To which saint is Westminster Abbey dedicated? **St Peter**

14. In the USA, what does the John Birch Society oppose? **Communism**

15. Would you find an escapement below a rampart, in a castle or in a clock? **In a clock**

16. What is the setting for the opera *Billy Budd*? **A warship**

17. What is the name of the boy in the *Winnie the Pooh* books? **Christopher Robin**

18. In which film does the character Oddjob appear? ***Goldfinger***

19. On which circuit is motor racing's Grand Prix d'Endurance run? **Le Mans**

20. Where in the body would you find a fontanelle? **In the skull**

Round 18

1. Where did the Yonghy Bonghy Bo live? **On the Coast of Coromandel (In the middle of the woods)**

2. Which adventure novel featured Gagool, Twala and Umbopa? ***King Solomon's Mines***

3. What was Coco Channel's Christian name? **Gabrielle**

4. Which American artist is famous for a picture of a can of beans? **Andy Warhol**

5. Which university did the prince attend in *The Student Prince*? **Heidelberg**

6. Does 'Chop Suey' literally mean bits and pieces, fried quickly or vegetable noodles? **Bits and pieces**

7. What is a dirndl? Is it a horse-drawn carriage, a dress, or a form of currency?   **Dress**

8. What was the occupation of Jack Ketch?   **Hangman**

9. True or false: Sir John Gielgud's first name was George.   **False (It was Arthur.)**

10. Who was Russian leader at the time of the Cuban crisis?   **Kruschev**

11. What was the first programme shown on Channel 4 on 2nd November 1982?   ***Countdown***

12. Which sport featured in the film *The Stratton Story*? Was it ice-hockey, drag-racing or baseball?   **Baseball**

13. Who succeeded Albert Reynolds as Prime Minister of Eire?   **John Bruton**

14. The Pindus Mountains run north to south through which country?   **Greece**

15. Which Shakespeare play includes the characters Petruchio, Katharina and Bianca?   ***The Taming of the Shrew***

16. Who said: "I've been accused of every death except the casualty list of the World War"?   **Al Capone**

17. Which pop group had a hit with *My Generation*?   **The Who**

18. From what is the brown pigment bistre prepared? Is it soot, cuttlefish ink or plant roots?   **Soot**

19. Who was known as the Iron Chancellor?   **Bismarck**

20. Which 16th century astrologer became famous for his obscure prophecies? **Nostradamus**

Round 19

1. Are Wu and Min pandas, languages or towns in Malaysia? **Languages**

2. Who played Commissioner Dreyfus in the *Pink Panther* films? **Herbert Lom**

3. Who swam the Hellespont every night to see his lover, Hero? **Leander**

4. Who was the first presenter of *The Golden Shot*? Was it Jackie Rae, Bob Monkhouse or Charlie Williams? **Jackie Rae**

5. In the nursery rhyme "*We are all in the dumps, For diamonds are trumps*", where have the kittens gone to? **St Paul's**

6. Which one word fits all these definitions: chemise, change of workmen, a trick and a typewriter key for making capitals? **Shift**

7. Which is the largest island just off the west coast of North America? **Vancouver Island**

8. Iodine is necessary for the functioning of which gland? **Thyroid**

9. Which American comedian, known for his meanness, had *Love in Bloom* as his signature tune? **Jack Benny**

10. Who played Toulouse Lautrec in the film *Moulin Rouge*? **José Ferrer**

11. Where do demersal creatures live? Is it in holes, on the seabed or on human skin?   **On the seabed**

12. In what year was the Battle of Agincourt?   **1415**

13. With what form of transport was Otto Lilienthal associated? Was it gliders, balloons or biplanes?   **Gliders**

14. Which Suffolk town, famous for an annual music festival, was the first town in Britain to have a woman mayor?   **Aldeburgh**

15. In which country is the source of the Amazon?   **Peru**

16. Whom did Anna Anderson claim to be?   **Anastasia**

17. What nationality was Anne of Cleves?   **German**

18. What is an army worm? Is it a snake, a millipede or a caterpillar?   **Caterpillar**

19. Which TV series made Jonathan Routh famous?   ***Candid Camera***

20. Who played Dr Phibes in two films?   **Vincent Price**

Round 20

1. True or false: the alpaca is a hoofed mammal?   **True**

2. Alum Bay, Godshill and Carisbrooke Castle are all in which county?   **Isle of Wight**

3. Who starred in the Oscar winning films *Quiet Please, The Little Orphan* and *The Milky Way*?   **Tom and Jerry**

4. Who was the leader of Zanu who became Zimbabwe's first president? **Robert Mugabe**

5. Is varicella the correct name for measles, chickenpox or shingles? **Chickenpox**

6. Where would you wear espadrilles? **On your feet**

7. The Sutherland Falls, among the highest in the world, are in Canada, New Zealand or India? **New Zealand**

8. Who composed *Clair De Lune*? **Debussy**

9. Who starred opposite Fred Astaire in the film *Easter Parade*? **Judy Garland**

10. Which battle of 1645 is said to have cost Charles I his throne? **Naseby**

11. In the Tarzan *stories*, what was the name of Tarzan's monkey friend? **Nkima**

12. Who was the courtier whom Dionysius of Syracuse seated beneath a sword suspended by a human hair? **Damocles**

13. Who was Millard Fillmore? Was he the inventor of Monopoly, the architect of Sydney Opera House or a US President? **US President (1850-52)**

14. What in history was referred to as Black Forty Seven? **Irish Potato Famine (1847)**

15. What was the name of Freddy Laker's cheap transatlantic air service of 1977? **Skytrain**

16. What name is given to the study of language sounds? **Phonetics**

17. True or false: Nancy Reagan was nicknamed The
    Smiling Mamba?   **True**

18. Which town is known as the capital of the
    Cotswolds?   **Cirencester**

19. Which religious movement was founded by John
    Thomas in 1848? Was it the Seventh Day Adventists,
    the Plymouth Brethren or the Christadelphians?
                              The Christadelphians

20. In which sport are there moves called Triffus, Miller
    and Rudolf?   **Trampolining**

Round 21

1. If Monday's child is fair of face, what is
   Wednesday's child?   **Full of Woe**

2. Who painted *Snow Storm – Steamboat off a
   Harbour's Mouth*?   **Turner**

3. What was the name of the decorative style of the
   1920s and 1930s characterised by geometrical
   designs and bright metallic surfaces?   **Art Deco**

4. In cricket, 111 is believed to be an unlucky score.
   What is it called?   **Nelson**

5. Who was the princess in *Sleeping Beauty*? Was she
   Aurora, Diana or Flora?   **Aurora**

6. Who led the British expedition which conquered
   Everest in 1953?   **John Hunt**

7. Who established the first English printing press in
   1476?   **William Caxton**

8. By what name is the flower Woodbine better known? **Honeysuckle**

9. Who is the central character in John Braine's book *Room At the Top*? **Joe Lampton**

10. What is the popular name for the constellation Crux? **Southern Cross**

11. Who beat Holland in the 1978 World Cup Final? **Argentina**

12. The John Gabel Entertainer appeared in California in 1906. Was it the player piano, the juke box, or the home film projector? **Juke Box**

13. True or false: there are 29 books in the New Testament? **False (27)**

14. When Michael Foale became the first Briton to walk in space, what first was achieved by his co-walker, Bernard Harris? **First black man to walk in space**

15. Which sport was founded in Britain on 28th August 1895? Was it Rugby League, Lawn Tennis or Speedway? **Rugby League**

16. In George Orwell's *1984* what is Britain called? Is it Oceania, Offshore or Airstrip One? **Airstrip One**

17. In which film did Julie Christie win an Oscar playing a model? ***Darling***

18. Which unit amalgamated with the Royal Flying Corps in 1918 to form the RAF? **Royal Naval Air Service**

19. In a famous case, which American spinster was accused of killing her parents in 1892? **Lizzie Borden**

20.   In which country was Lady Astor, first woman MP
      to enter the Commons, born? Was it Canada,
      America or Australia?   **America**

Round 22

1.   Which famous greyhound, first to win the
      Greyhound Derby twice, won 46 of his 61 races?
                                          Mick the Miller

2.   Where was the poet standing when he was inspired
      to write the poem beginning "Earth has not
      anything to show more fair"?   **Upon Westminster
                                              Bridge**

3.   What was Barbara Castle's parliamentary
      constituency?   **Blackburn**

4.   Who, in the Sermon on the Mount, did Jesus warn
      would appear as wolves in sheep's clothing?   **False
                                              Prophets**

5.   A talbot was often seen in heraldic designs. Was it a
      griffin, a lion rampant or a dog?   **Dog**

6.   In which former abbey in Devon can you see
      Drake's Drum?   **Buckland**

7.   In mythology, what was odd about Cassandra's
      prophecies?   **Nobody believed them**

8.   Who played Gloria in *It Ain't Half Hot, Mum*?
                                          Melvyn Hayes

9.   True or false: Shelley wrote "To err is human, to
      forgive divine"?   **False (Pope did.)**

10. What kind of plant is fescue? Is it a grass, a fern or a moss? **Grass**

11. What 'remedy', of no medicinal value, is given to humour a patient? **Placebo**

12. Who became King of England in 1100? **Henry I**

13. What is the capital of the Canadian province of Alberta? **Edmonton**

14. What was the name of the first yacht to win the America's Cup? *America*

15. What is the common name for the scapula? **Shoulder Blade**

16. Is a margay a plant, a tiger-cat or a wave in permed hair? **Tiger-cat**

17. Who was known as The Forces Sweetheart? **Vera Lynn**

18. Which washerwoman did Arthur Lucan play in 14 films and on stage? **Old Mother Riley**

19. Who fronted and devised the TV show *It's A Square World*? **Michael Bentine**

20. What is the relationship between Prince Andrew and Lord Lindley? **They are cousins**

Round 23

1. What is Daley Thompson's first name? **Francis**

2. Who had No 1 hits with *Can the Can* and *Devil Gate Drive*? **Suzi Quatro**

3.   Which aircraft, piloted by Gary Powers, was shot
     down by Russia on 1st May 1960?   **U-2**

4.   Who was Jeanette MacDonald's singing partner in
     many musical films?   **Nelson Eddy**

5.   True or false: Operation Overlord was the
     code-name for Germany's invasion of Russia?
                        False (Overlord was D-Day.)

6.   Who wrote the biography of Dr Johnson?   **James
                                              Boswell**

7.   Which British city was the first to erect a monument
     to Lord Nelson? Was it Hereford, Edinburgh or
     Glasgow?   **Glasgow**

8.   On which river does Canterbury stand?   **Stour**

9.   Which monarch wrote the Casket Letters?   **Mary,
                                         Queen of Scots**

10. Which Christian name is applied to a plane's
     automatic pilot?   **George**

11. Which Oscar winning film of the 1980s was directed
     by Hugh Hudson?   ***Chariots of Fire***

12. Who played the title role in *The Wizard of Oz*?
                                    Frank Morgan

13. Which chief led the resistance against the Romans
     in 43 AD? Was it Caractacus, Prasutagus or
     Madoc?   **Caractacus**

14. Which American people were the first to drink
     cocoa?   **The Aztecs**

15. Who played Dr Cameron in the TV series *Dr
     Finlay's Casebook*?   **Andrew Cruickshank**

16. In which American state is the Garden of the Gods?
Colorado

17. Which British football club is known as The Bhoys?
(Glasgow) Celtic

18. By what name was broadcaster Derek McCulloch better known?
Uncle Mac

19. Who made her first appearance in *Murder at the Vicarage*?
Miss Marple

20. Which is the largest theatre in the West End? Is it the Palladium, the Old Vic or the Coliseum?
Coliseum

Round 24

1. Who became MP for Falmouth and Camborne in 1992?
Sebastian Coe

2. True or false: cockfighting was banned in 1899?
False (1849)

3. The book subtitled *The Contemplative Man's Recreation* is concerned with what pastime?
Angling

4. Who devised the package tour?
Thomas Cook

5. Who played the lead in the TV series *Sorry*?
Ronnie Corbett

6. Which group had albums called *Fireball* and *Machine Head*?
Deep Purple

7. To what was Sir Walter Scott referring when he wrote: "Full well I love thy mixed and massy piles."?
Durham Cathedral

8. Later to be Mrs McAliskey, who became MP for
    Mid Ulster in 1969?   **Bernadette Devlin**

9. Who played the title role in the film *The Prime of
    Miss Jean Brodie*?   **Maggie Smith**

10. What kind of notice puts a block on the publication
    of information in the interests of security?   **D notice**

11. Where can the letters DG REG FD be seen every
    day?   **On coins**

12. Who wrote: "The female of the species is more
    deadly than the male."? Was it Kipling, Wilde or
    Pope?   **Kipling**

13. What was the nickname of the British 7th
    Armoured Division in World War 2?   **Desert Rats**

14. Which type of bullet was outlawed in 1899?
                    Dum Dum

15. With which instrument was Jacqueline Du Pré
    associated?   **Cello**

16. Which programme was presented on radio by Roy
    Plomley from 1942 to 1985?   ***Desert Island Discs***

17. What is the other name of the sword sometimes
    called Caliburn?   **Excalibur**

18. True or false: the Battle of Edgehill was in 1645?
                    False (1642)

19. In which story are Ralph, Jack and Peterkin
    shipwrecked on a desert island?   ***The Coral Island***

20. Who is the most famous child of Prince Andrew
    of Greece and Princess Alice of Battenburg?
                    Prince Philip

Round 25

1. Who played the Jackal in the film *The Day of the Jackal*? **Edward Fox**

2. With what is the society called EXIT concerned? Is it Euthanasia, Emigration or Divorce? **Euthanasia**

3. Which pop singer and actor was born Terry Nelhams? **Adam Faith**

4. When Argentinians landed on South Georgia in 1982 what had they supposedly come to collect? **Scrap metal**

5. What was the name of the dog in Enid Blyton's *Famous Five* books? Was it George, Timmy or Monty? **Timmy**

6. Which Hampshire air show is held biennially in September? **Farnborough**

7. Which British boxer lost to Joe Louis on points in 1937 when fighting for the World Heavyweight Title? **Tommy Farr**

8. Who conducted the famous TV interview series *Face To Face*? **John Freeman**

9. Who coined the phrase "a land fit for heroes to live in"? Was it Asquith, Bonar Law or Lloyd George? **Lloyd George**

10. Whose collected plays were published in the *First Folio*? **Shakespeare's**

11. Which pop group was formed by Roy Wood in 1971 and had No 1 albums with *Time* and *Discovery*? **ELO**

12. Who was the bully in the book *Tom Brown's Schooldays*?   **Flashman**

13. What was the name of Harry Llewellyn's gold-medal-winning horse in the 1952 Olympics?   **Foxhunter**

14. True or false: Edward I's wife was called Isabella?   **False (Eleanor or Margaret)**

15. Which poet is buried in Grasmere churchyard?   **Wordsworth**

16. Which city did the Romans call Glevum? Was it Gloucester, Glasgow or Liverpool?   **Gloucester**

17. Which Treasury Minister was murdered by an IRA bomb outside his home in 1990?   **Ian Gow**

18. In which comedy TV series did Ballard Berkeley play Major Gowen?   ***Fawlty Towers***

19. For what was Beryl Grey famous? Was it Opera, Ballet or Sculpture?   **Ballet**

20. What did Sir Lancelot's adultery prevent him from doing?   **Finding the Holy Grail**

Round 26

1. Who played the title role in *Gandhi* in 1982?   **Ben Kingsley**

2. The current Duke of St Albans is a direct descendant of Charles II's mistress. Who was she?   **Nell Gwynn**

3. Which sea lies between the Bosporus and the Dardanelles?   **Sea of Marmara**

4. Who became Nelson's mistress and bore him a child in 1801? **Lady Hamilton**

5. Who wrote *The Good Companions*? Was it G B Shaw, J B Priestley or Oscar Wilde? **J B Priestley**

6. Which handicapped physicist wrote *A Brief History of Time*? **Stephen Hawking**

7. With what does *Grove's Dictionary* deal? Is it the clergy, music or word derivations? **Music**

8. Which literary family lived at Haworth in Yorkshire? **The Brontës**

9. Tartan Khan, I'm Slippy and Tico have all won what famous race? **Greyhound Derby**

10. True or false: there are no Victorian Teddy Bears? **True (First one in 1902)**

11. Which famous dancing troupe was formed by Margaret Kelly? **Bluebell Girls**

12. Who hosted the radio quiz show *Have a Go*? **Wilfrid Pickles**

13. Which Public School's school song begins: "Forty years on, when far and asunder"? **Harrow**

14. In which famous adventure story is Harry Faversham the central character? ***The Four Feathers***

15. What is a gibus? Is it a collapsible top hat, a type of monkey or an ancient sailing ship? **Collapsible top hat**

16. In which part of the British Isles would you find bailiwicks? **Channel Isles**

17. How long is a dog watch at sea? **Two hours**

18. What legal-sounding name is given to a temporary mast rigged at sea?   **Jury mast**

19. Which murderer lived at 10 Rillington Place?
                                        John Christie

20. What product did Mary Holland spend 18 years advertising on TV?   **Oxo**

Round 27

1. Who made the first cross-Channel flight in 1909?
                                        Louis Blériot

2. In which film did Tom Cruise take Dustin Hoffman to Las Vegas?   ***Rain Man***

3. Where was the German fleet scuttled in 1919?
                                        Scapa Flow

4. Who had a mountain retreat at Berchtesgaden?
                                        Hitler

5. Whose only No 1 hit was *Barbados* in 1975?
                                        Typically Tropical

6. How many named people went to Widdicombe Fair with Uncle Tom Cobbleigh and the singer?   **Six**

7. In *Brookside*, who was buried under the patio?
                                        Trevor Jordache

8. Who wrote *The Count of Monte Cristo*?   **Alexandre Dumas**

9. True or false: Hughie Greene presented the TV series *Take Your Pick*?   **False (It was Michael Miles.)**

10. Which people worshipped the rain god Apu Ilapu? Was it the Cherokee, the Incas or the Mongols?
The Incas

11. What sort of creature was Chewbacca in *Star Wars*?
A Wookey

12. What was the name of Emile Ford's backing group?
The Checkmates

13. How often does the phoenix rise from the ashes?
Every 500 years

14. Which capital city's name means 'meeting of the muddy waters'? Is it Kuala Lumpur, Rangoon or Bangkok? **Kuala Lumpur**

15. What is your columella? Is it the tip of your ear, your eyelid or the skin that separates your nostrils?
Skin separating nostrils

16. What makes stainless steel stainless? **Chromium**

17. In which city is the Fitzwilliam Museum?
Cambridge

18. Whose address was No 1, London? Was it Gladstone's, the Duke of Wellington's or George I's? **Duke of Wellington's**

19. What was the main wood used by Thomas Chippendale in the 18th century? Was it rosewood, boxwood or mahogany? **Mahogany**

20. In what year was poison gas used in war for the first time? Was it 1915, 1916 or 1917? **1915**

Round 28

1. In 1926 Gertrude Ederle was the first woman to do what?   **Swim the English Channel**

2. From which animal does cashmere come?   **A goat**

3. In the Sci Fi novel *Fahrenheit 451* what did firemen do?   **Burn books**

4. Which film star's biography was called *Neither Shaken Nor Stirred*?   **Sean Connery**

5. True or false: Casanova was Italian?   **True**

6. In which country would you be if you landed at Dalaman airport?   **Turkey**

7. The mythical creature a silkie, is half man half . . . (what)?   **Seal**

8. What was the official residence of British sovereigns from 1698 until 1837?   **St James's Palace**

9. Off which South American port was the Graf Spee scuttled in 1939?   **Montevideo**

10. What is the name of the big cannon in Edinburgh Castle?   **Mons Meg**

11. Which word means one tenth of a nautical mile?
                                                          Cable

12. What is the minimum age a US President has to be?
                                                              35

13. If you were lapidated, what would happen to you?
                                            Stoned to death

14. Which was the first British National Park?   **Peak District**

15. Apart from Galahad, two other knights achieved
    the Holy Grail. Name one.   **Bors or Percival**

16. Which chemical element is found in all proteins? Is
    it carbon, oxygen or nitrogen?   **Nitrogen**

17. Which fruit has the Latin name prunus persica? Is it
    the peach, the plum or the damson?   **Peach**

18. What nationality was the composer Rachmaninov?
                                                Russian

19. A musket ball fired from the French ship
    Redoubtable killed which famous Englishman?
                                            Lord Nelson

20. What would you expect in a pluvial region?   **Rain**

Round 29

1. True or false: St Austell is in Cornwall?   **True**

2. Who was the first negro boxer to be World
   Heavyweight Champion?   **Jack Johnson**

3. What attracted many Americans to the Sioux's
   sacred Black Hills in the 1860s?   **Gold**

4. After sheltering from a storm near Cheddar
   Gorge, Augustus Toplady wrote which hymn?
                                        Rock of Ages

5. What was the title of the book about the Watergate
   scandal written by Washington Post reporters
   Bernstein and Woodward?   ***All the President's Men***

6. In the film *Who Framed Roger Rabbit?*, what was
   Roger's wife called?   **Jessica**

7.   You would use dannocks if you were hedging.
      What are they?   **Thick gloves**

8.   Where is the Chester Beatty Library? Is it in Perth,
      Dublin or Cardiff?   **Dublin**

9.   In what capacity did the writer Ernest Hemingway
      serve in World War 1?   **Ambulance Driver**

10.   Who broke Roger Bannister's mile record?   **John
                                                      Landy**

11.   Schnauzer is a breed of which animal?   **Dog**

12.   Who wrote the music for the ballet *Les Sylphides*?
      Was it Chopin, Tchaikovsky or Mozart?   **Chopin**

13.   In which city are the Spanish Steps?   **Rome**

14.   Who was the oldest woman to sit in the House of
      Commons? Was it Bessie Braddock, Irene Ward or
      Barbara Castle?   **Irene Ward**

15.   What is kelp?   **Seaweed**

16.   How long did Mary Poppins say she would stay
      with the children?   **Until the wind changed**

17.   True or false: Andrew was the brother of Simon,
      called Peter?   **True**

18.   Metric crown, metric demy and metric royal are
      different sizes of what?   **Paper**

19.   What name is sometimes given to the legislative
      assembly of a country that is derived from the Latin
      for old man?   **Senate**

20.   Who dined on mince and slices of quince?   **The Owl
                                               and the Pussycat**

Round 30

1. If you ordered pamplemousse in a French restaurant, what would you get? **Grapefruit**

2. From the 14th century to 1830 the eldest sons of French kings were known by what title? **Dauphin**

3. After Pacific, Atlantic and Indian, which is the next largest ocean? **Arctic**

4. Why was General Claus von Stauffenberg executed in 1944? **He tried to assassinate Hitler**

5. What is the name for food permissible under Moslem dietary laws? **Halal**

6. Which saint's cathedral is in Moscow's Red Square? **St Basil's**

7. With which sport is Wayne Gretzky associated? **Ice Hockey**

8. Marble is formed by the metamorphosis of which rock? Is it limestone, sandstone or granite? **Limestone**

9. Which English composer wrote a *Sea Symphony* and a *London Symphony*? **Ralph Vaughan Williams**

10. Where did methyl isocyanate cause 2,600 deaths in 1984? **Bhopal in India**

11. How many cards are there in a tarot pack? Is it 64, 72 or 78? **78**

12. What character was played by Peter Sellers in the film *I'm Alright, Jack*? **Fred Kite**

13. In which city was Europe's first hard paste porcelain made? Was it Dresden, Worcester or Meissen?   **Dresden**

14. Who had No 1 hits with *Tired of Waiting For You* and *Sunny Afternoon*?   **Kinks**

15. Who wrote the book *Schindler's Ark*?   **Thomas Kenneally**

16. What is the name of the bass tuba that wraps around the player's body?   **Sousaphone**

17. Which is the largest English national park? Is it Dartmoor, Exmoor or the Lake District?   **Lake District**

18. Who said: "There are only two kinds of music; good and bad."?   **Duke Ellington**

19. Which acid builds up in the muscles during strenuous exercise?   **Lactic Acid**

20. True or false: Utah is nicknamed The Waterfall State?   **False (Beehive State)**

Round 31

1. Who was the little boy brought up by wolves in *The Jungle Book*?   **Mowgli**

2. Who was King of France at the time of the French Revolution?   **Louis XVI**

3. What makes green pasta green? Is it broccoli, cabbage or spinach?   **Spinach**

4. What is the name for a person who will eat no food of animal origin?   **Vegan**

5. Which element is found in bones, teeth and shells?
    Calcium

6. Which pop singer played the title role in the film
    Tommy? **Roger Daltrey**

7. What is a booby? Is it a tropical fish, a tropical bird
    or a tropical lizard? **Tropical bird**

8. The playwright Pirandello wrote a play called *Six
    Characters In Search Of An* . . . . . (what)? *Author*

9. Is the Great Wall of China 1250, 1450 or 1650 miles
    long? **1450 miles**

10. Who first said: "A week is a long time in politics."?
    Harold Wilson

11. Who has produced CDs called *Tell Mama*, *Seven
    Year Itch* and *Stickin' To My Guns*? **Etta James**

12. Is an apse a poisonous snake, part of a church or an
    acidic fruit? **Part of a church**

13. What kind of wild cattle with shaggy coats and
    upturned horns live in the mountains of Tibet?
    Yaks

14. Which carbohydrate makes jam gel? **Pectin**

15. Who had Top Ten hits in the 1960s with *Calendar
    Girl*, *I Go Ape* and *Little Devil*? **Neil Sedaka**

16. True or false: a manometer measures the pressure of
    liquids? **True**

17. Which record producer created the 'Wall of Sound'
    for the Crystals and Ronettes? **Phil Spector**

18. After which frontier scout was the capital of
    Nevada named? **Kit Carson**

19. Which river flows for 1500 miles through Venezuela, forming part of the border with Colombia? Is it the Amazon, the Orinoco or the Rio de la Plata?   **The Orinoco**

20. What would you use if you practised ikebana?
                                                   Flowers

Round 32

1. What type of novels were written by Zane Grey?
                                                    Westerns

2. Which animals were dachshunds originally bred to hunt?   **Badgers**

3. Who played the witch-wife in the TV series *Bewitched*?   **Elizabeth Montgomery**

4. Which many-headed monster's blood killed Hercules?   **Hydra**

5. What is the collective name for rain, snow, hail and sleet?   **Precipitation**

6. In which Italian city is Michelangelo's statue of David? Is it Florence, Venice or Rome?   **Florence**

7. Which famous American's two year old son was kidnapped and murdered in 1932?   **Charles Lindbergh's**

8. Who had a 1966 hit with *Good Vibrations*?   **Beach Boys**

9. With what is the Birkenhead Drill concerned?
                        Women and children first in lifeboats

10. Which medical device was invented by Dr Rene Laennec to preserve his female patients' modesty?
Stethoscope

11. Which part of the body contains the choroid, sclera and fovea? **Eye**

12. True or false: Sir Robert Helpmann was Australian? **True**

13. Which Italian expression meaning 'in the church style' denotes unaccompanied singing? **A cappella**

14. Whom did Achilles kill and drag round Troy behind his chariot? **Hector**

15. Which is the fifth book of the New Testament?
Acts of the Apostles

16. Which flavouring is added to brandy and egg yolks to make advocaat? Is it aniseed, zest of an orange or vanilla? **Vanilla**

17. What colour is a kingfisher's egg? **White**

18. Which part of the body is affected by osteomyelitis?
Bones

19. Was Wright of Derby a painter, a porcelain maker or a soap manufacturer? **Painter**

20. What is a durmast? Is it a fruit, a tree or a songbird?
Tree (oak)

Round 33

1. In which art form did German born Ernst Lubitsch gain fame? **Cinema**

2.   Which is Poland's largest river? Is it the Oder, the
      Dvina or the Vistula?   **Vistula**

3.   Which boxer's real name was Walker Smith?
                                      Sugar Ray Robinson's

4.   Which was the first Harry Palmer film?   ***The
                                            Ipcress File***

5.   In which city did Anne Frank write her diary?
                                            Amsterdam

6.   Edward de Vere, 17th Earl of Oxford, is claimed by
      some as the real author of what?   **Shakespeare's
                                               works**

7.   Who set stories in the imaginary county of
      Barsetshire?   **Anthony Trollope**

8.   True or false: Catherine Parr never re-married
      after Henry VIII's death?   **False
                (She married Thomas Seymour.)**

9.   Which Top Ten hit of 1962 contained these lines:
      "There's more than 7 wonders in this world: I've
      just met No 8."?   ***Venus in Blue Jeans***

10.   Who wrote the TV series *Curry and Chips*?   **Johnny
                                               Speight**

11.   What is the family name of the Dukes of
      Northumberland?   **Percy**

12.   With which country do you associate Test cricketer
      Heath Streak?   **Zimbabwe**

13.   Which artist painted 62 self portraits? Was it Van
      Gogh, Rembrandt or Picasso?   **Rembrandt**

14.   Which writer created The Saint?   **Leslie Charteris**

15. What is xerography? Is it writing about foreigners, the x-ray process or photocopying?   **Photocopying**

16. John Bellingham shot and killed whom in the House of Commons in 1812?   **Spencer Perceval**

17. Who was King Solomon's mother?   **Bathsheba**

18. Which war began on June 25th, 1950?   **Korean**

19. Who played the police chief in the film *Jaws*?   **Roy Scheider**

20. *The Outlaw*, *The Conqueror*, *The Good* and *The Fourth* were all descriptions in the titles of books about which rascal?   **William Brown**

Round 34

1. On which river is Balmoral Castle?   **Dee**

2. When was the wearing of front seat belts made compulsory? 1982, 1983 or 1984?   **1983**

3. Which is the lightest known substance?   **Hydrogen**

4. True or false: XCI are the Roman numerals for 111?   **False (91)**

5. Whom did Sherlock Holmes refer to as THE Woman?   **Irene Adler**

6. What was the major event that took place at Golgotha?   **Christ's crucifixion**

7. What would you do with a futon? Would you eat it, wear it or sleep on it?   **Sleep on it**

8. Which English playwright was murdered by his lover, Kenneth Halliwell, in 1967?   **Joe Orton**

9. Whose *Born In the USA* album was a massive bestseller in 1985? **Bruce Springsteen's**

10. Which animal was traditionally called 'Russell'? **Fox**

11. Which English queen died of smallpox at the age of 32? **Mary II**

12. Which German city was the target of the first 1000-bomber raid? Was it Dresden, Hamburg or Cologne? **Cologne**

13. Which creatures collect in a clowder? **Cats**

14. How long does it take the Earth to travel one and a half million miles? Is it a day, a week or a month? **A day**

15. In which country is Transylvania? **Romania**

16. Which character did David Jason play in *Porridge*? **Blanco**

17. Who won the Women's London Marathon in 1984 and 1985? **Ingrid Christianson**

18. In which English city was the first Salvation Army brass band formed? Was it Derby, Oxford or Salisbury? **Salisbury**

19. Which international footballer is commemorated in two stained-glass windows at St Francis's Church in Dudley, near his home? **Duncan Edwards**

20. Which American played a teacher in the film *Ryan's Daughter*? **Robert Mitchum**

Round 35

1. True or false: the Stretford End is at Edgbaston? **False (Old Trafford)**

2. Who was the last prisoner to be held in the Tower of London? **Rudolf Hess**

3. In which book did people find Shangri-La? *Lost Horizon*

4. Which amber globe was named after a 1930s' Minister of Transport? **Belisha Beacon**

5. What did baker John Faynor's carelessness cause? **The Fire of London**

6. Who played M in the Bond film *Goldeneye*? **Judi Dench**

7. Where is the most famous colony of Macaque Monkeys? **Gibraltar**

8. Captain Bligh was elected a fellow of the Royal Society for services to what? **Navigation and botany**

9. Which punk musician's real name was Simon Ritchie? **Sid Vicious**

10. Who drew the Mister Men? **Roger Hargreaves**

11. From whom did the animals seize the farm in *Animal Farm*? **Mr Jones**

12. Which creature's Latin name is *bufo bufo*? **Toad**

13. What is the correct name for the high jump event in showjumping? **Puissance**

14. Which ship sent the first SOS? *Titanic*

15. When was decimal currency introduced in Britain? **1971**

16. What was the name of Guy Gibson's dog?   **Nigger**

17. True or false: a VLCC is an oil tanker?   **True**

18. Is a belvedere a bluebell, a viewing turret or an old name for a badger?   **Viewing turret**

19. Into which river did the Pied Piper lead the rats? Was it the Elbe, Rhine or Weser?   **Weser**

20. What is the common name for the psychological Rorschasch Test?   **Ink blot test**

Round 36

1. What is the capital of Australia?   **Canberra**

2. In *Dad's Army* what was Private Fraser's daytime job?   **Undertaker**

3. Which wine is flavoured with pine resin?   **Retsina**

4. Which of these plants produces most food per acre? Is it pineapple, banana or melon?   **Banana**

5. Which horse won the Derby, St Leger and 2000 Guineas in 1970?   **Nijinsky**

6. Which literary character's main opponent was Von Stalhein?   **Biggles**

7. Who married the Earl of Bothwell in 1567?   **Mary, Queen of Scots**

8. Which proboscis has 40,000 muscles?   **An elephant's trunk**

9.   Which American developed a talent as a great
     short-story writer while serving time in prison for
     embezzlement?   **O Henry**

10. Which Tolstoy heroine threw herself under a train?
                                            Anna Karenina

11. In medieval art, what did a dog signify? Was it
     ferocity, fidelity or friendship?   **Fidelity**

12. Whose last words, allegedly, were: "I've had 18
     straight whiskies, I think that's a record."?   **Dylan
                                                    Thomas**

13. Which British poet is revered as a hero in Greece?
                                                    Byron

14. True or false: a normal piano has 88 keys?   **True**

15. Name one of the two bridges under which the crews
     pass in the University Boat Race?   **Hammersmith
                                              or Barnes**

16. A size 9 man's shoe in Britain is what in the USA?
                                                       10

17. In mythology, who blinded Polyphemus?   **Ulysses**

18. Which Psalm's first line is: "The Lord is my
     shepherd, I shall not want"?   **Psalm 23**

19. What does a philogynist like?   **Women**

20. Who had a No 1 hit in 1981 with *Tainted Love*?
                                                 Soft Cell

Round 37

1.   Which island merged with Tanganyika to form a
     new country in 1964?   **Zanzibar**

2. Who became British Prime Minister in 1945?
    Clement Attlee

3. On TV, who presented *This Is Your Life* in 1995?
    Michael Aspel

4. Which Frenchman created the character of
    Monsieur Hulot?   **Jacques Tati**

5. In the Tarzan novels, what does 'Tarzan' mean? Is
    it Ape Man, White Skin or Jungle King?   **White
    Skin**

6. Which singer's catchphrase was "You ain't heard
    nothing yet"?   **Al Jolson's**

7. Which Republic currently exists in France?   **The
    Fifth**

8. Tupamaros are guerillas in which country? Is it
    Brazil, Chile or Uruguay?   **Uruguay**

9. Which one word fits these definitions: sensitive or
    delicate, offer or present, easily chewed?   **Tender**

10. Who wrote the songs *Jambalaya*, *Your Cheating
    Heart*, *Hey, Good Lookin'* and *Cold Cold Heart*?
    Hank Williams

11. If you sailed west from Land's End and followed
    the same line of latitude, which country would you
    reach first?   **Canada**

12. After India became independent, dispute over
    which state led to a war with Pakistan?   **Kashmir**

13. What would you do with kvass? Would you eat it,
    drink it or paint it?   **Drink it**

14. Who was Olympic Men's 400 Metres champion in
    1992?   **Quincy Watts**

15. What nationality was the artist Albrecht Dürer?
    Was he Belgian, Dutch or German?   **German**

16. True or false: the University of Essex is based in
    Colchester?   **True**

17. Why was 29 a fateful number for Mrs Beeton,
    Anne Boleyn, Carole Landis and Percy Shelley?
    All died aged 29

18. From which country did Israeli commandoes
    rescue 106 hijacked air passengers in 1976?
    Was it Lebanon, Egypt or Uganda?   **Uganda**

19. What was Christopher Dean's job before he
    became a professional skater?   **Policeman**

20. In which sport would you go to a basho?   **Sumo
                                              wrestling**

Round 38

1. Who, in films, played Hans Christian Andersen
   and the trumpeter Red Nicholls?   **Danny Kaye**

2. What does the prefix 'crypto' mean?   **Secret,
                                              unknown**

3. Which country's international car registration
   letters are PL?   **Poland**

4. Who played Ada in *For the Love of Ada*?   **Irene
                                                Handl**

5. Where would you find a daglock? In a canal, on a
   sheep's rear end or in a safe?   **On a sheep's rear end
                                (dirt covered clump of wool)**

6.   How many years of marriage are indicated by a china wedding anniversary?   **20**

7.   How many decibels is the average whisper? Is it 5, 10 or 20?   **20**

8.   Which gangster was shot dead by the FBI on 22nd July 1934 as he came out of the Biograph Cinema in Chicago?   **John Dillinger**

9.   Who wrote *To the Lighthouse* and *Mrs Dalloway*?   **Virginia Woolf**

10. Who captained Spurs when they did the double in 1961?   **Danny Blanchflower**

11. What is the legal name for a spoken or written insult against religious belief or sacred objects?   **Blasphemy**

12. True or false: a cord is a measure of cut wood?   **True**

13. What was Bing Crosby's first name?   **Harry**

14. Which Irish novelist was unable to walk or stand until he was 17, and then became an outstanding athlete and footballer at Dublin University?   **Bram Stoker**

15. What was banned in the USA by the 18th Amendment?   **Alcohol**

16. Where were Geoff Hamilton's BBC gardens?   **Barnsdale**

17. Which famous American folksinger had the first names Woodrow Wilson?   **Woody Guthrie**

18. Which Canadian city was devastated in 1917 when an ammunition ship blew up in the harbour?   **Halifax**

19. In which country did the 1976 Jonestown massacre occur? Was it Guyana, USA or Guatemala?
Guyana

20. Which is the largest city in China?   **Shanghai**

Round 39

1. Who led the junta which seized the Falklands in 1982?   **Galtieri**

2. In which county is Romney Marsh?   **Kent**

3. On which island is Mount Suribachi?   **Iwo Jima**

4. Who played King Feisal of Iraq in the film *Lawrence of Arabia*?   **Alec Guinness**

5. Which bandleader married Lana Turner and Ava Gardner? Was it Stan Kenton, Woody Herman or Artie Shaw?   **Artie Shaw**

6. Which planet has satellites called Miranda, Ariel, Puck and Desdemona?   **Uranus**

7. During World War 2 Norman Shelley was enlisted to imitate whom in radio broadcasts?
Winston Churchill

8. Which Englishman was murdered outside the Dakota Building in New York in 1980?   **John Lennon**

9. True or false: Italy joined the EEC in 1958?   **True**

10. Which doctor performed the first human heart transplant?   **Christiaan Barnard**

11. What was the subject of the 1963 Beeching Report?
                                              Railways

12. Who wrote *The Forsyte Saga*?   **John Galsworthy**

13. Who played Sir Lancelot Spratt in the *Doctor* films?
                                    James Robertson Justice

14. Who painted the famous picture of Guernica,
     bombed in the Spanish civil war?   **Picasso**

15. Which MP said: "I married beneath me – all
     women do."?   **Nancy Astor**

16. In Russia, what was a gulag?   **Prison Camp**

17. Name Reg Holdsworth's mother-in-law.   **Maud
                                              Grimes**

18. What is the correct collective name for a litter of
     piglets?   **Farrow**

19. The adjective 'costal' applies to which part of the
     body?   **Ribs**

20. Phnom Penh is capital of which country?   **Cambodia**

Round 40

1.   Which Irish tenor was so admired and respected that
     he was made a Papal count?   **John McCormack**

2.   In which city are the US football team The
     Redskins based?   **Washington**

3.   What colour flag is flown at beaches deemed clean
     and pollution-free?   **Blue**

4.   What is the capital of New Zealand?   **Wellington**

5. Which film family were introduced in the 1947 film *Holiday Camp*? **The Huggetts**

6. Which judge presided at the infamous Bloody Assizes in 1685? **Judge Jeffreys**

7. Which one word means a poultry disease, a fruit's seed and a spot on a die? **Pip**

8. Which famous literary duo first appeared together in the story *The Man with Two Left Feet*? **Bertie Wooster and Jeeves**

9. What is the positive heavy particle of an atom's nucleus? Is it the proton, neutron or electron? **Proton**

10. In which sport did Phil Read win many World Championships? **Motor Cycling**

11. Which TV series featured Lord and Lady Brightlingsea, Lord Seadown and Helmsley Thwaite? *The Buccaneers*

12. What is the correct name for larceny from a consecrated building? **Sacrilege**

13. Which country's king was the Prisoner of Zenda? **Ruritania's**

14. Who would use a trochee? A poet, a surgeon or an engineer? **A poet**

15. Of what did Prince Albert die? **Typhoid fever**

16. What would you do with a zinfandel? Wear it, play it or make wine with it? **Make wine**

17. What is British Honduras now called? **Belize**

18. True or false: the largest island in Asia is Sumatra?
False (Borneo)

19. Ipoh, Kuching, Johore Bahru and Georgetown are all towns in which Commonwealth country?
Malaysia

20. What nationality was Boutros Boutros Ghali, Secretary General of the UN? **Egyptian**

Round 41

1. The French ship *Petit Pierre* was the first to be driven (in 1902) by what? Was it a propellor, a diesel engine or a steam turbine? **Diesel engine**

2. In what field did Walter Gropius achieve fame?
Architecture

3. For what is the Prix Goncourt awarded? Is it music, cinema or literature? **Literature**

4. In what year was Lord Mountbatten murdered? Was it 1977, 1978 or 1979? **1979**

5. In which game would you use the expression 'J'adoube'? **Chess**

6. By what name did Rose Louise Hovick achieve fame? **Gypsy Rose Lee**

7. What is the currency of Argentina? **Peso**

8. In films, who played Captain Bligh, Henry VIII and Quasimodo? **Charles Laughton**

9. Who was the first Prime Minister of Israel? **David Ben-Gurion**

10. Of which country was Ferdinand Marcos President from 1965 to 1986? **Philippines**

11. In Russia, what is Kyzyl Kum? Is it a gigantic crater, a huge lake or a desert? **Desert**

12. Who landed at Le Bourget airport on May 21st, 1927? **Charles Lindbergh**

13. Which country has Colombia to the west and Guyana to the east? **Venezuela**

14. True or false: China is the world's top fishing nation in tonnage? **True**

15. Which famous English comedy star was born blind but gained his sight after a fit of coughing? **George Formby**

16. In which country do the Walloons live? **Belgium**

17. For what sort of activity was Sir Francis Walsingham, Elizabeth I's Secretary of State, best remembered? **Espionage**

18. Which musical note has half the value of a crotchet? **A quaver**

19. Which sport is believed to have originated on Pentecost Island as an initiation ceremony? **Bungee Jumping**

20. Which word is used in radio call signs for Y? **Yankee**

Round 42

1. With which identification system is Francis Galton associated? **Fingerprints**

2. Where was Joan of Arc burnt at the stake? **Rouen**

3. What does etymology deal with?   **Word origins**

4. Who played Ratso Rizzo in the film *Midnight Cowboy*?   **Dustin Hoffman**

5. Who is reckoned to have invented bifocal lenses?   **Benjamin Franklin**

6. In which daily newspaper does Rupert the Bear appear?   *Daily Express*

7. What colour is puce? Is it orange yellow, purple brown or light red?   **Purple Brown**

8. Where did the Confederates surrender in 1865? Was it Gettysburg, Richmond or Appomattox?   **Appomattox**

9. On TV, what one word connects these characters? Martin Platt, Kate Wilson and Gladys Emmanuel?   **Nurse**

10. True or false: the Yucatan Peninsula is in Honduras?   **False (Mainly in Mexico)**

11. Who plays Jean-Luc Picard in *Star Trek – The Next Generation*?   **Patrick Stewart**

12. In which film did John Wayne use a group of boys on a cattle drive?   *The Cowboys*

13. Who succeeded Henry VIII as monarch?   **Edward VI**

14. Which Spanish artist's most famous painting was *The Persistence of Memory*?   **Dali's**

15. In which country was Alfredo di Stefano of Real Madrid born? Was it Argentina, Spain, or Colombia?   **Argentina**

16. What name is given to a joint of beef cut from the breast next to the ribs? **Brisket**

17. In which US state are The Everglades? **Florida**

18. What would you do with a filibeg? Play it, fight with it or wear it? **Wear it**

19. In which sea are the Dodecanese Islands? **Aegean Sea**

20. In what year was the first decimal coin circulated in Britain? **1969**

Round 43

1. From which planet does Dr Who come? **Gallifrey**

2. In 1994 the Chinese sporting World Champions Lu Bin and Yang Aihua tested positive for drugs. In what sport were they world champions? **Swimming**

3. Who wrote *Dr Zhivago*? **Boris Pasternak**

4. Which swashbuckling star starred in the silent films *The Three Musketeers*, *Robin Hood* and *The Black Pirate*? **Douglas Fairbanks**

5. Which one word can mean a parasitic worm, the hook of an anchor and a lucky chance? **Fluke**

6. True or false: the organisation RIBA is for architects? **True**

7. What is measured in bathyl, abyssal and hadal zones? Is it the density of stars, mountain crevasses or ocean depths? **Ocean depths**

8. Which is the world's oldest stock exchange? Is it
    Antwerp, Hamburg or Amsterdam?   **Antwerp**

9. True or false: Georgetown is the capital of
    Barbados?   **False (It's Bridgetown.)**

10. On TV, whose stooges have included Rodney
    Bewes, Derek Fowlds and Roy North?   **Basil
    Brush**

11. Who played Tommy Steele in the film *The Tommy
    Steele Story*?   **Tommy Steele**

12. Who was Wimbledon Women's Singles Champion
    in 1994?   **Conchita Martinez**

13. In Jewish folklore, who is Lilith?   **A Demon or
    Adam's first wife**

14. What does a myologist study? Is it fungi, muscles or
    mosses?   **Muscles**

15. Which performer was shown on the Ed Sullivan
    Show only from the waist up?   **Elvis Presley**

16. Who wrote *All Quiet On the Western Front*?   **Erich
    Remarque**

17. Which is the world's largest computer
    manufacturer?   **IBM**

18. Which detective was helped by Steve?   **Paul Temple**

19. Which animal caused the death of William III?
    Mole

20. From which musical does the song *Goodbye* come?
    White Horse Inn

Round 44

1. Near which British seaside resort are the Great and
    Little Ormes?   **Llandudno**

2. Which pop group named itself after a 1956 John
    Wayne film?   **The Searchers**

3. Which plant's Latin name is *Ficus Elastica*? Is it the
    rubber plant, aspidistra or ivy?   **Rubber plant**

4. In World War 2 what name was given to the
    German technique of sending U-Boats out in
    groups?   **Wolf Pack**

5. True or false: Muslims have to pray 7 times a day?
                                             False (5 times)

6. Kohoutek, Tempel-Tuttle and Halley's are all
    what?   **Comets**

7. The Chinese call it the Huang Ho. What do we call
    it?   **Yellow River**

8. The 1984 TV drama *Threads* showed a nuclear
    bomb falling on which British city?   **Sheffield**

9. What calibre should a firearm be to be classed as
    artillery? Over 10mm, 20mm or 30mm?   **Over
                                                    20mm**

10. Who married Bianca de Macias on 12th May 1971?
                                               Mick Jagger

11. What is a bullace? Is it a fruit, a fish or a bird?
                                                     Fruit

12. Where in Britain is the Neolithic village of Skara
    Brae?   **The Orkneys**

13. Which game originated in India under the name *Caturanga*? **Chess**

14. The battle of Vittoria in 1813 was the last battle in which war? **Peninsular War**

15. Into which sea does the River Jordan flow? Is it the Mediterranean, the Red or the Dead? **The Dead Sea**

16. Which group had hits with *Mr Tambourine Man* and *Eight Miles High*? **The Byrds**

17. Who played Philo Beddoe in two films? **Clint Eastwood**

18. Which Mexican revolutionary, first name Emiliano, was assassinated in 1919? **Zapata**

19. Which singer was given the nickname The Killer? **Jerry Lee Lewis**

20. Which is South Africa's *administrative* capital? Is it Cape Town, Bloemfontein or Pretoria? **Pretoria**

Round 45

1. True or false: George Washington was a surveyor before becoming a soldier? **True**

2. Who played Ironside on TV? **Raymond Burr**

3. To a sailor especially, what is a hawser? **A rope**

4. Which kingdom was ruled by Herod the Great? **Judaea**

5. What was the profession of John Dunlop, who patented the pneumatic tyre in 1888? Was he a cart maker, an accountant or a veterinary surgeon?
Veterinary surgeon

6. What did Jason and the Argonauts seek? **The Golden Fleece**

7. What name is shared by an Asian capital, a Canadian provincial capital and an African lake? **Victoria**

8. During prohibition, what name was given to an illegal drinking club? **Speakeasy**

9. Wat Arun, The Temple of the Dawn, is in which capital city? **Bangkok**

10. What was the name of Richard Beckinsale's character in *Porridge*? **Lennie Godber**

11. In which sport were Tramontona British Champions from 1986 to 1989? (Black Bears and Hildon have been more recent winners.) **Polo**

12. Which people's name means "eaters of raw meat"? **Eskimoes**

13. Who played The Forger in the film *The Great Escape*? **Donald Pleasence**

14. Who wrote *The Sea Wolf* and *White Fang*? **Jack London**

15. With what is a thanatologist concerned? Is it death, the sea or hidden treasure? **Death**

16. Which animal is sometimes said to be 'in velvet'? **Deer**

17. True or false: *The Two Towers* is a book in *The Lord of the Rings* trilogy? **True**

18. Which leader wrote his thoughts in a little red book?   **Chairman Mao**

19. In 1707, which English admiral was thrown ashore when his flagship, *Association*, sank off the Scilly Isles, and was murdered by a woman for the great ring on his finger?   **Cloudesley Shovell**

20. Which word, derived from Polynesian, means forbidden or prohibited?   **Taboo**

Round 46

1. Who was Olympic Boxing Light Heavyweight Gold medallist in 1960?   **Cassius Clay**

2. Tau, omicron, epsilon and lambda are all found where?   **In the Greek alphabet**

3. The discovery of the Babington Plot led to the death of which monarch?   **Mary, Queen of Scots**

4. In which country are Europe's only wild bison?   **Poland**

5. Which mythical creature was the symbol of virginity?   **Unicorn**

6. In which film is this the last line: "Tomorrow is another day."?   ***Gone With The Wind***

7. Which ex-England goalkeeper was killed in the Munich air crash?   **Frank Swift**

8. Which monkeys are known for their blue and red faces and buttocks?   **Mandrills**

9. Who played the female lead in the *Ghostbusters* films?   **Sigourney Weaver**

10. What was the name of King Arthur's treacherous nephew?   **Modred (or Mordred)**

11. Which animal lives in a citadel? Is it a weasel, a mole or a badger?   **Mole**

12. Which group released an album called *Lexicon of Love*?   **ABC**

13. True or false: Paul Newman's wife is Joanne Dru?
    False (It is Joanne Woodward.)

14. On TV, which holiday camp is featured in the series *Hi De Hi*?   **Maplins**

15. In which war was the Battle of Antietam?
    American Civil War

16. Which Labour weekly did Michael Foot edit for nine years?   *Tribune*

17. Rulers of which ancient civilisation wore a double crown to signify the unification of the Upper and Lower kingdoms?   **Egypt**

18. Which was the first British pop group to tour China?   **Wham**

19. F Murray Abraham won Best Actor Oscar for his part in which musical film biography?   *Amadeus*

20. Of what is petrology the study?   **Rocks**

Round 47

1. Who founded the National Viewers and Listeners Association?   **Mary Whitehouse**

2.   Imran Khan played cricket for Worcestershire and which other English county?   **Sussex**

3.   Where are calderas found? On the sea bed, in kitchens or on the tops of volcanoes?   **On the tops of volcanoes**

4.   Which character appears in the most Shakespeare plays?   **Falstaff**

5.   In which sport did Richard Meade win Olympic gold?   **Equestrianism – 3 day event**

6.   Which common object has an inertia reel?   **Car seat belt**

7.   What name is given to a cow's first milk after calving? Is it bedew, bennets, or beestings?   **Beestings**

8.   Name one of Britain's allies in The Seven Years War.   **Prussia or Hanover**

9.   True or false: Nicolas Soult was one of Napoleon's generals?   **True**

10. What number do the Roman numerals MDXCV represent?   **1595**

11. Which comedian and *That's Life* presenter was famous for his odd odes?   **Cyril Fletcher**

12. What character did Paul Eddington play in *Yes, Minister*?   **Jim Hacker**

13. In one word, what is yeast?   **(A) fungus**

14. Who described foxhunting as "the unspeakable in pursuit of the uneatable"?   **Oscar Wilde**

15. In London, what was the Tyburn? A stream, the gallows or an arch?   **A stream**

16. The Cod Wars of the 1970s were between Britain and which country? **Iceland**

17. In Norse mythology, who was the evil and mischievous god? **Loki**

18. Who killed Macbeth in Shakespeare's play?
Macduff

19. Which is the loudest insect? Is it a cricket, a cicada or a blow fly? **Cicada**

20. For what purpose did the Mayan people build pyramids? Was it as tombs, temples or palaces?
Temples

Round 48

1. Who was detective Sexton Blake's assistant?
Tinker

2. Where would you be if you ate al fresco? **Outside, in the open air**

3. Who lost the battle of Ulm in 1805? Was it Prussia, Austria or Russia? **Austria**

4. What is the plural of axis? **Axes**

5. True or false: Melbourne is the state capital of Victoria? **True**

6. Who is the leading character of the story that has a fairy called Tinker Bell? **Peter Pan**

7. What word is used to describe descending a sheer face by sliding down a doubled rope? **Abseiling**

8. What was found buried at Sutton Hoo in 1939? **A Saxon ship**

9. Which magical character was played by Gudrun Ure on TV in 1985? **Supergran**

10. On which river does Belfast stand? Is it the Liffey, Lagan or Lough? **Lagan**

11. In which US state are the Green Mountains? **Vermont**

12. Which physical property allows a needle to float on water? **Surface tension**

13. Which one word means a type of sandpiper, an Elizabethan collar and to trump at cards? **Ruff**

14. Which common substance is made by boiling down horns, hides and hoofs? **Glue**

15. Who won Best Actor Oscar in 1989 for *My Left Foot*? **Daniel Day-Lewis**

16. If your face was rugose, what would it be? **Wrinkled**

17. What type of music is produced by French speaking settlers of Louisiana? **Cajun**

18. In Arthurian legend, what was Ron? Was it Arthur's spear, shield or horse? **Spear**

19. In which country was the governor or viceroy called The Khedive from 1867 to 1914? **Egypt**

20. If you carry out bel canto, what are you doing? **Singing**

Round 49

1. True or false: Lionel Hampton played the tenor saxophone? **False (He played the vibraphone.)**

2. In which county is the naval base of Gosport? **Hampshire**

3. Who played the camp commandant in the TV series *Colditz*? **Bernard Hepton**

4. Who said about sex: "The whole thing is like finding a frog in a coffee jar."? **Stephen Fry**

5. What part of your body would interest a rhinologist? **Nose**

6. Which country lies between Zimbabwe and the sea? **Mozambique**

7. Which 'ruler' died of a "bastard tertian ague" in 1658 and later his body was mistreated? **Oliver Cromwell**

8. What pachydermic nickname is given to a gift or possession which is useless and expensive to maintain? **White Elephant**

9. Which bird is used in a squab pie? **Pigeon**

10. What is grown in a paddy field? **Rice**

11. Red, fennec, Arctic and bat-eared are all species of which animal? **Fox**

12. Spell Desiccated. **Desiccated**

13. In what game could you have a pone: Mah Jong, backgammon or cards? **Cards (Player to right of dealer who cuts the cards.)**

14. Which Government Department is responsible for broadcasting and the media, the arts, sport and recreation?   **National Heritage**

15. The ancient figure called a fylfot or gammadion became better and more threateningly known to us as what?   **Swastika**

16. What was the name of the butler in the TV series *To the Manor Born*?   **Brabinger**

17. True or false: a futtock is a ship's timber?   **True**

18. In a famous Beckett play, for whom were Vladimir and Estragon waiting?   **Godot**

19. From which country did Paddington Bear come?
                                                              Peru

20. Which new watersport was added to the Olympics in 1984?   **Synchronised swimming**

Round 50

1. In which popular TV series did a character called Seymour Atterthwaite appear for one series?
                                          Last of the Summer Wine

2. Which word means to turn a ship on one side for cleaning and caulking?   **Careening**

3. In the famous poem, who stole the green eye of the little yellow god?   **Mad Carew**

4. Where in London is the American Embassy?
                                            Grosvenor Square

5. Which Danish player played for Newcastle United when they won the Fairs Cup?   **Ben Arentoft**

6.   In which film did Robert Redford and Jane Fonda play newly weds who lived on the top floor of a liftless apartment building?   ***Barefoot In the Park***

7.   What name was given to the programme of social reform attempted by President Truman?   **Fair Deal**

8.   What name in the Bible means 'He who strives with God' and was the name given to Jacob after he'd wrestled with an angel?   **Israel**

9.   What is the supreme goal of Buddhists?   **Nirvana**

10.   Which country issued a 12d black stamp in 1851? Was it Britain, Australia or Canada?   **Canada**

11.   With which ancient people would you associate The Book of the Dead?   **Egyptians**

12.   If you suffer from comedones, what have you got?   **Blackheads**

13.   From which film did Stevie Wonder's *I Just Called To Say I Love You* come?   ***The Woman in Red***

14.   Who wrote the novel *Fair Stood the Wind For France*?   **H E Bates**

15.   In which Shakespeare play do suitors have to choose from three caskets for the hand of the heroine?   ***The Merchant of Venice***

16.   In which sport did Wilt Chamberlain and Alton Byrd achieve fame?   **Basketball**

17.   Which group would you associate with *Light My Fire*, *Hello I Love You* and *Riders On the Storm*?   **The Doors**

18.   Who was *The Once and Future King* written about by T H White?   **King Arthur**

19. What do you use if you foretell the future by conchomancy?   **Shells**

20. Who was the first presenter of TV's *Tomorrow's World*?   **Raymond Baxter**

Round 51

1. Who was described as 'the mouse that built an empire'?   **Mickey Mouse**

2. What is the Church of England's smallest administrative unit?   **A parish**

3. Who played John in the TV series *Dear John*?   **Ralph Bates**

4. What was Marilyn Monroe's character name in *Some Like It Hot*?   **Sugar Kane**

5. Who, in a famous monologue by Stanley Holloway, was swallowed by a lion at Blackpool Zoo? Was it Sam, Albert or Charley?   **Albert**

6. Which people's creation legend is told in the Dreamtime Stories?   **Australian Aborigines'**

7. Who put Sweeney Todd's victims into her pies?   **Mrs Lovett**

8. Which pop group released the albums *White Light, White Heat* and *Loaded*?   **Velvet Underground**

9. The adjective 'cutaneous' refers to which part of the body? Is it the nails, the blood vessels or the skin?   **Skin**

10. In films, who played the Thin Man?   **William Powell**

11. Where in Britain did the Battle of the Beanfield
     occur in 1985?   **Stonehenge**

12. What is added to mineral water to make tonic
     water?   **Quinine**

13. What first ran from Paddington to Farringdon
     Street in 1863?   **London Underground**

14. What is the collective name for a group of mice?
                                               Nest

15. In the nursery rhyme, what would be Curly Locks'
     only work?   **To sew a fine seam**

16. True or false: the *Torrey Canyon* was a Kuwaiti oil
     tanker?   **True**

17. Who wrote the book *Mussolini, His Part in My
     Downfall*?   **Spike Milligan**

18. In which county was John Major's constituency in
     the 1992 General Election?   **Cambridgeshire**

19. What was called the jewel in Queen Victoria's
     crown?   **India**

20. Which plant was believed to shriek when pulled up?
                                            Mandrake

Round 52

1. What is pargeting? Is it a system of roof tiling,
    glazed porcelain or a type of plastering?   **A type of
                                                 plastering**

2. Who played Ingrid Bergman's husband in
    Casablanca?   **Paul Henreid**

3. If you had a gigot would you play it, eat it or wear

it?   **Eat it**

4. Which cereal is used in Scotch Broth?   **Barley**

5. Who had Top Ten hits in the1980s with *Wouldn't It Be Good*, *The Riddle* and *Wide Boy*?   **Nik Kershaw**

6. Which islands did Captain Cook name the Friendly Islands?   **Tonga**

7. Which TV series featured the *Daily Crucible* newspaper?   ***Hot Metal***

8. How many unions merged to form Unison in 1993? Was it 3, 4 or 5?   **3**

9. Which story and film were inspired by a World War 2 shipwreck off the island of Barra?   ***Whisky Galore***

10. Matlock is the administrative centre of which county?   **Derbyshire**

11. Who was head of the German SS?   **Himmler**

12. True or false: Anthony Trollope wrote *Tom Brown's Schooldays*?   **False (Thomas Hughes did.)**

13. Which holes at deck level in a ship's sides let water drain away?   **Scuppers**

14. In which radio series did Osric Pureheart appear?
    Crazy People **(and** *The Goon Show*)

15. Who composed *Putting on the Ritz*, *Easter Parade* and *God Bless America*?   **Irving Berlin**

16. Who founded the Free Presbyterian Church of Ulster in 1951?   **Ian Paisley**

17. Blue Vinney is a type of what? Is it quartz, cheese or moss?   **Cheese**

18. Which ex-soldier wrote *The Seven Pillars of Wisdom*?   **T E Lawrence (Lawrence of Arabia)**

19. Who was Russian Foreign Minister from 1957 to 1985?   **Gromyko**

20. Who appeared in these films: *From Here To Eternity*, *Suddenly Last Summer*, *Red River* and *The Misfits*?
        Montgomery Clift

Round 53

1. Who played The Virginian on TV?   **James Drury**

2. When were Nobel Prizes first awarded? Was it 1901, 1905 or 1909?   **1901**

3. What are auctioned at Tattersalls?   **Racehorses**

4. Who was the youngest general in the American Civil War?   **George A Custer**

5. With which sporting or leisure activity was Edward Whymper associated?   **Mountaineering**

6. Which musical includes the songs *Gee, Officer Krupke* and *America*?   ***West Side Story***

7. Who on TV presented the Arts programme *Monitor* and was Director General of BBC TV from 1968 to 1975?   **Huw Wheldon**

8. True or false: film star Ray Milland was born in Wales?   **True**

9. Who played Glenn Miller's wife in *The Glenn Miller Story*?   **June Allyson**

10. What is the state capital of South Carolina?
        Columbia

11. Which organisation's motto is "Courtesy and
    Care"?   **The Automobile Association's**

12. Which controversial Oliver Stone film starred Woody
    Harrelson as Mickey?   *Natural Born Killers*

13. For what was John Singer Sargent famous? Was he
    a painter, writer or composer?   **Painter**

14. Who won the Nobel Prize for chemistry the year
    after Marie Curie died? Was it her husband, her
    daughter or her son?   **Her daughter**

15. Which legendary ship is doomed to sail forever?
                                The Flying Dutchman

16. Which cartoonist created St Trinian's?   **Ronald
                                                  Searle**

17. What sort of music did Ira D Sankey compose?
                                        Hymns

18. Which English city is named after Snot and his
    tribe?   **Nottingham**

19. Who wrote the *Gormenghast Trilogy*?   **Mervyn
                                                Peake**

20. "A day that shall live in infamy." What is the exact
    date of that day?   **7th December 1941
    (The Japanese attack on Pearl Harbor.)**

Round 54

1. In what year was Princess Margaret married? Was
   it 1959, 1960 or 1963?   **1960**

2. Which TV sexy serial featured a model called *Sugar
   Bush*?   *Black Eyes*

3. Which inventor's first film (one minute long) was called *Fred Ott's Sneeze*? **Edison's**

4. True or false: Harold Macmillan met Ian Smith on board HMS *Tiger* in 1966? **False (Harold Wilson did.)**

5. Which country's soldiers might wear a stiff skirt called a fustanella? **Greece's**

6. Who was the last English king to die in battle? **Richard III**

7. Who starred in the silent films *Blood and Sand*, *The Eagle* and *The Sheik*? **Rudolph Valentino**

8. Which is the ancestral home of the Dukes of Bedford? **Woburn Abbey**

9. What was Tom's job in *The Water Babies*? **Chimney Sweep**

10. Alchemists sought for an object that would turn base metals into gold. What did they call this imaginary object? **Philosopher's Stone**

11. Who is the mother of James Ogilvy? **Princess Alexandra**

12. Which film star published his autobiography in three volumes, including *Snakes and Ladders* and *Orderly Man*? **Dirk Bogarde**

13. Which cartoon character was 'the fastest mouse in all Mexico'? **Speedy Gonzales**

14. Who could only play one tune – *Over the hills and far away*? **Tom, the piper's son**

15. Which African president was assassinated at a military review in 1981? **President Sadat of Egypt**

16. What has a testatrix done?	**Made a will**

17. What is the popular name for toxaemia?	**Blood Poisoning**

18. In legend, what was the name of King Arthur's fairy sister?	**Morgan Le Fay**

19. Which sci-fi film featured three robots called Huey, Louie and Dewey?	***Silent Running***

20. Who said about oral contraception: "I asked this girl to sleep with me and she said 'No.' "?	**Woody Allen**

Round 55

1. Which shipwrecked sailor settled a war between King Bombo and King Little?	**Gulliver**

2. Who was the father of the disciples James and John?	**Zebedee**

3. Which county's motif is a standing bear next to a ragged staff?	**Warwickshire**

4. Whose four wives included Ann Howe and Miranda Quarry?	**Peter Sellers**

5. Which is the last of the year's four Quarter days?	**Christmas Day**

6. Which terrier is the largest of the terrier breeds?	**Airedale**

7. Which bear protected Mowgli in *The Jungle Book*?	**Baloo**

8. Which comedian's catchphrase was "Can you hear me, Mother?"?	**Sandy Powell**

9. Where was the first British Grand Prix held in 1926?
Brooklands

10. Which branch of mathematics deals with the relationship between the sides and angles of triangles? **Trigonometry**

11. Where does the Lutine Bell hang? **Lloyds of London**

12. Who played the central character in the film *The Loneliness of the Long Distance Runner*? **Tom Courtenay**

13. What is a turnstone? Is it an ore, a bird or a flower? **A bird**

14. Who wrote the plays *Bar Mitzvah Boy* and *Spend, Spend, Spend*? **Jack Rosenthal**

15. Which Trojan's story is told in the *Aeneid* by Virgil? **Aeneas**

16. In a nursery rhyme, where would you go to see a fine lady with bells on her toes? **Banbury Cross**

17. What was the title of the first women's magazine, published in 1693? **The Ladies' Mercury**

18. How many points does a compass have? **32**

19. In which 1984 film did Sean Connery return as James Bond after a thirteen year gap? **Never Say Never Again**

20. What is the last event in the Decathlon? **1500 metres**

Round 56

1. What does a hippophobe fear?   **Horses**

2. What is the collective name for a group of leopards?
   A leap

3. In the film *When Harry Met Sally*, who played
   Harry?   **Billy Crystal**

4. Who played the radio talk-show host in TV's
   Midnight Caller?   **Gary Cole**

5. Which one word fits these definitions: to transplant,
   bribery and hard work?   **Graft**

6. Which type of music, popular in the1950s, featured
   washboard, tea chest bass and other improvised
   instruments?   **Skiffle**

7. What do you need to sup with the devil?   **A long
   spoon**

8. Who warned Julius Caesar to beware the Ides of
   March in Shakespeare's play?   **A soothsayer**

9. What was snooker referee Len Ganley advertising
   when he crushed a snooker ball to powder?
   Carling Black Label

10. According to an old rhyme, what does a sneeze on
    Wednesday signify?   **A letter**

11. Who rush in where angels fear to tread?   **Fools**

12. Who was Rudolph Raspe's baron who told such
    tall stories?   **Munchausen**

13.   Which English king was murdered at Berkeley Castle, traditionally by the insertion of a red hot iron into his body so that no external marks would be visible?   **Edward II**

14.   Which group had Top Ten hits with *Dancing Party*, *I Wonder Why* and *A Little Bit of Soap*?
                                            Showaddywaddy

15.   Who played Test cricket for England in 1930 when he was 52 years old?   **Wilfred Rhodes**

16.   True or false: the *Flying Hamburger* was a diesel train?   **True**

17.   Which element has the Atomic Number 1?
                                                Hydrogen

18.   Who had hits with *Homeward Bound*, *I Am a Rock* and *The Boxer*?   **Simon and Garfunkel**

19.   What is the name for a right-hander's off break delivered with a leg break action?   **Googly**

20.   What important compound was found on the Moon in 1998?   **Water**

Round 57

1.   What is jingoism?   **Excessive patriotism**

2.   Which water gate lies under St Thomas's Tower in the Tower of London?   **Traitor's Gate**

3.   In a famous story, who was Passepartout's master?
                                            Phileas Fogg

4.   Which empire builder's last words were: "So little done; so much to do."?   **Cecil Rhodes's**

5. Who won Best Actress Oscars for *Dangerous* and
    Jezebel?   **Bette Davis**

6. Who played The Charmer in the TV series of the
    same name?   **Nigel Havers**

7. Which gangleader's men were murdered in the St
    Valentine's Day Massacre? Was it Bugs Moran's,
    Legs Diamond's or Dutch Schultz's?   **Bugs Moran's**

8. Which one word fits all these definitions: rubbish,
    drugs and a boat?   **Junk**

9. What does a haematologist study?   **The blood**

10. Which criminal was made into a romantic figure by
    the novel *Rookwood*?   **Dick Turpin**

11. Which snake appears on the crown of Egyptian
    Pharaohs?   **Cobra**

12. True or false: Jainism is an ancient religion?   **True**

13. What is the capital of Bolivia?   **La Paz**

14. Which star of the *Folies-Bergère* adopted a 'rainbow'
    family of children of different nationalities?
                                            Josephine Baker

15. Who painted *Derby Day* and *The Railway Station*?
    Was it Constable, Frith, or Rossetti?   **Frith**

16. What is said to be the mother of invention?
                                                 Necessity

17. In which TV series did Donna Reed step into
    Barbara Bel Geddes' shoes?   *Dallas*

18. Who won the Women's Olympic 100 metres in
    1992?   **Gail Devers**

19. In the UK, excluding mainland Britain, what is the largest island? Is it the Isle of Wight, Lewis with Harris or Skye?   **Lewis with Harris**

20. Who had Top Ten hits in the 1980s with *Something About You*, *Lessons in Love* and *Running in the Family*?   **Level 42**

Round 58

1. Which bubble burst in 1720 and caused a financial panic?   **The South Sea Bubble**

2. Which US poetess married Ted Hughes and committed suicide aged 31?   **Sylvia Plath**

3. Near which North American city are the Plains of Abraham?   **Quebec**

4. Which great film star's last film was *Cuban Rebel Girls* in 1959?   **Errol Flynn**

5. Which Bishop signs himself Roffen?   **Bishop of Rochester**

6. What did Perseus's helmet do for him?   **Made him invisible**

7. The original Charing Cross was erected to commemorate Edward I's queen. What was her name?   **Eleanor**

8. True or false: Dr Maria Montessori was an advocate of family planning?   **False (She was an educationalist.)**

9. Elvis Presley had three successive No 1 hits in the UK charts in 1961. Name one.   *Are You Lonesome Tonight*, *Wooden Heart*, or *Surrender*

10. Who played Mrs Robinson in the film *The Graduate*? **Anne Bancroft**

11. Near which Bavarian city did the Nazis hold huge rallies in the 1930s? **Nuremberg**

12. What form did the Egyptian god Sebek take? Was it a jackal, crocodile or hippopotamus? **A crocodile**

13. How many Olympics have been cancelled due to war? **Three**

14. Who wrote the novels *Rabbit, Run*, *Rabbit Redux* and *Rabbit Is Rich*? **John Updike**

15. In ballet, what does plié mean? Is it bending the body, bending the legs or bending the arms? **Bending the legs**

16. In the 1980s, who was the only non-American or European to win the Ladies' Singles at Wimbledon? **Evonne Cawley**

17. Who was Penny's boyfriend in *Just Good Friends*? **Vince**

18. Whom did the British, under Allenby, defeat at the Battle of Megiddo in World War 1? **The Turks**

19. What name was given to the first complete Bible printed in America and published in 1663? **The Indian Bible**

20. What is the administrative HQ of Hampshire? **Winchester**

Round 59

1. Which Gospel writer has the lion as his symbol? **Mark**

2. What is the term which means using a gentler expression to soften a blunt one? **Euphemism**

3. Which one word means very thin sheet metal, to baffle or thwart and a blunt sword? **Foil**

4. True or false: the Red Laws were a civil code of ancient Athens? **False (They were the Civil Code of Ancient Rome.)**

5. What is baccarat? **A card game**

6. Who created the naval character Hornblower? **C S Forester**

7. Which of the big cats have tear stain facial markings? **Cheetahs**

8. Who had Top Ten hits in the 1960s with *Together*, *Somewhere* and *Hold Me*? **P J Proby**

9. Who was the father of Henry I? Was it William I, Stephen or John? **William I**

10. In which TV series did Googie Withers play prison governess Faye Boswell? ***Within These Walls***

11. Steve Hislop won which trophy several times on a Honda? **Isle of Man TT Trophy**

12. With which children's TV programme would you associate Zippy, George and Bungle? ***Rainbow***

13. Which famous military group has its HQ at Aubagne near Marseilles? **Foreign Legion**

14. Which actress was stabbed in the shower in *Psycho*? **Janet Leigh**

15. The T-34, M-4 and Pz III were all what? **Tanks**

16. Which New Zealand writer created Roderick Alleyn of Scotland Yard? **Ngaio Marsh**

17. What was the trade name of the construction kits, introduced in 1907, consisting of metal strips with holes, screws, nuts, bolts, etc? **Meccano**

18. What is the magical kingdom in *The Lion, the Witch and the Wardrobe*? **Narnia**

19. Which US President's Presidency was called the Thousand Days? **J F Kennedy's**

20. True or false: Jimmy Nail reached No 1 with *Love Don't Live Here Anymore*? **False (No 3)**

Round 60

1. What is a fedora? **A hat**

2. Where is the Prado Art gallery? **Madrid**

3. Who anointed Saul and David as Kings of Israel? Was it Eli, Samuel or Daniel? **Samuel**

4. Which disease is carried by bark beetles? **Dutch Elm Disease**

5. What was Bruce Channel's No 2 hit in 1962? *Hey! Baby*

6. In Greek mythology, who was the messenger of the gods? **Hermes**

7. What is tansy? Is it a bird, a herb or a disease? **Herb**

8. Elmo Lincoln, Gene Polar, Jock Mahoney and Mike Henry have all played which screen hero? **Tarzan**

9. How many players are there on each side in Australian Rules Football? Is it 14, 16 or 18?   **18**

10. Who played the title character in the TV series *My Wife Next Door*?   **Hannah Gordon**

11. What are tested in the Trial of the Pyx ceremony?   **Coins of the realm**

12. In which county is Hemel Hempstead?   **Hertfordshire**

13. In the Bible, who wrote most of the Epistles?   **St Paul**

14. In cricket, who scored England's first Test century?   **W G Grace (1880)**

15. What does QU stand for in QUANGO?   **Quasi**

16. True or false: Garbo's last film was *Two-Faced Woman*?   **True**

17. What is kohlrabi?   **A vegetable (cabbage)**

18. Who or what would make use of musits or musets?   **A hare (They are the gaps in a hedge through which a hunted hare escapes.)**

19. What sort of animal is a Lippizaner?   **A horse**

20. Who played the title role in the film *The Millionairess*?   **Sophia Loren**

Round 61

1. How many years are there in a millennium?   **1000**

2. Which great bird carried off Sinbad the Sailor?   **Roc or Rukh**

3. Which was the first country to win the Football World Cup in its own country? **Uruguay**

4. Who starred in the films *The Execution of Private Slovik*, *Badlands* and *Out of the Darkness*? **Martin Sheen**

5. Which American wrote *Astoria*, *The Legend of Sleepy Hollow* and *Bracebridge Hall*? **Washington Irving**

6. Was Charlie Chaplin's middle name Winston, Spencer or Burroughs? **Spencer**

7. Which country has the International Vehicle Registration Letter C? **Cuba**

8. Who had Top Ten hits with *Red Light Spells Danger*, *Suddenly* and *Caribbean Queen*? **Billy Ocean**

9. In the 19th century, what were Piccadilly Weepers? Were they knee ribbons, false eyelashes or droopy whiskers? **Droopy whiskers**

10. In *The Pardoner's Tale*, for what did the three rioters go looking? **Death**

11. Which sport is enjoyed by the Leander Club? **Rowing**

12. Who played Raffles in the TV series of the same name in the 1970s? **Anthony Valentine**

13. Which animals collect in a crash? **Rhinoceroses**

14. In which city is Schiphol airport? **Amsterdam**

15. What is the official language of Dominica? **English**

16. True or false: Cambrai was a battle in the First World War? **True**

17. What was a ducat? **A coin**

18. In which city is the famous marble bridge called the Rialto? **Venice**

19. You would find information on what in *Debrett's*? **The Peerage**

20. Who played the male lead in *Blood Alley*, *The High and the Mighty* and *In Harm's Way*? **John Wayne**

Round 62

1. Which song begins: "Alas my love, you do me wrong to cast me off discourteously"? ***Greensleeves***

2. Who was court painter to Charles I? Was it Holbein, Van Dyck or Gainsborough? **Van Dyck**

3. Who connects *The Student Prince*, the TV series *Sword of Freedom* and *The Egyptian*? **Edmund Purdom**

4. Whom did Harold II succeed to the English throne? **Edward the Confessor**

5. Which famous novel has the characters the Cheeryble Brothers, Mulberry Hawk, Madeline Bray and Newman Noggs? ***Nicholas Nickleby***

6. With which sport are Bob Falkenberg, Dick Savitt and Ted Schroeder associated? **Tennis**

7. Who played Charlie Endell in *Budgie*? **Iain Cuthbertson**

8. What does the Glorious First of June commemorate? **A sea battle**

9. Who had Top Ten hits with *Got To Give It Up*, and *Abraham Martin and John*? **Marvin Gaye**

10. In which country do 100 kobo equal 1 naira? Is it Nigeria, Ghana or Sierra Leone? **Nigeria**

11. With what was the Triangular Trade chiefly concerned? **Slaves**

12. True or false: the Zeppelin airship was never in commercial service? **False (1910-1914)**

13. Which black basalt slab, found by Napoleon's soldiers in Egypt, was the key to the translation of Egyptian hieroglyphic writing? **The Rosetta Stone**

14. Which king led the Huns from 445 to 450 AD? **Attila**

15. What was the name for the wooden head of a woman with a clay pipe in her mouth at fairs and at which people threw wooden balls? **Aunt Sally**

16. What is a taipan? An alligator, a snake or a boat? **A snake**

17. Which term for Ireland was first used by Dr Drennan in his poem *Erin*? **Emerald Isle**

18. Which Irish ghost is said to wail outside houses where a death is imminent? **Banshee**

19. Which one word means dry wine, to discharge and a hemp bag? **Sack**

20. Which actor was torn between Sigourney Weaver and Melanie Griffiths in *Working Girl*? **Harrison Ford**

Round 63

1. What, in the building trade, is called 'harling' in Scotland? **Pebble dash or rough cast**

2. Who had Top Twenty hits with *Legs* and *Gimme All Your Lovin'* and a No 22 with *Sharp-Dressed Man*? **ZZ Top**

3. Which Archbishop of Canterbury, who had supported Henry VIII's claim to be head of the Church of England, was burnt at the stake in 1556? **Thomas Cranmer**

4. In economics, according to Gresham's Law, what does bad money do? **Drives out good**

5. In which novel did Catherine Earnshaw marry Edgar Linton? **Wuthering Heights**

6. Adam Bell, Clym of the Clough and William of Cloudesley were all famous what? **Archers**

7. Where in London would you see the White Tower? **Tower of London**

8. True or false: the town of Blarney is in County Donegal? **False (It is in Cork.)**

9. Which footballer became the then record signing for a transfer deal between two English clubs on January 10th, 1995? **Andy Cole**

10. What began as the Christian Mission in Whitechapel in 1865? **Salvation Army**

11. What sort of guides were published by George Bradshaw? **Railway**

12. In which country was Andrew Carnegie born: Scotland, New Zealand or USA? **Scotland**

13. How many archangels are named in the Book of Enoch: 7, 13 or 99? **7**

14. Which hero married Bedr-el-Budur? Was it Aladdin, Ali Baba or Alexander the Great? **Aladdin**

15. Whose Top Ten hits included *What Is Love?*, *New Song* and *Pearl in the Shell*? **Howard Jones'**

16. Who scored the last goal in the 1966 Football World Cup final? **Geoff Hurst**

17. Which crimefighter was played by Peter Weller in a 1987 film? **Robocop**

18. Which novel features Colonel Creighton, Hurree Babu and Mahbub Ali? *Kim*

19. In Norse mythology, what was Bifrost? Was it a giant tree, an eight-legged horse or a rainbow bridge? **A rainbow bridge**

20. What was the name of the character played by Ann Mitchell in *Widows* and *She's Out*? **Dolly Rawlins**

Round 64

1. In which hills is Cheddar Gorge? **Mendips**

2. Who, in the Bible, was the youngest son of Jacob? **Benjamin**

3. In cricket, what do the Australians call extras? **Sundries**

4. True or false: Sir Walter Scott wrote a novel called *The Black Dwarf*? **True**

5. Who made a Biblical riddle out of bees nesting in a
    dead lion?   **Samson**

6. What was unusual about the Roman consul
    Incitatus?   **He was a horse**

7. What does a cricket umpire signal by raising one
    arm horizontally?   **No Ball**

8. Who made an album called *Highway 61 Revisited*?
                                          Bob Dylan

9. Which animal is Canada's official emblem?   **Beaver**

10. For every seven white keys on a piano, how many
    black keys are there?   **Five**

11. What is the green-eyed monster?   **Jealousy**

12. In ancient days, what was a carrack? Was it a
    barrel, a ship or a weapon?   **A ship**

13. In which game are flattened iron rings thrown
    at a hob?   **Quoits**

14. Which country's official name is Daehan (or
    Taehan) Minkuk (or Minguk)?   **South Korea**

15. Who played Danny Kaye's leading lady in three
    films, James Cagney's wife in *White Heat* and Burt
    Lancaster's love interest in *The Flame and the
    Arrow*?   **Virginia Mayo**

16. Which tough guy actor's last film was *The
    Carpetbaggers*?   **Alan Ladd's**

17. With which instrument is Max Roach associated?
                                             Drums

18. Who had Top Ten hits with *Don't Answer Me*,
    Conversations and *It's For You*?   **Cilla Black**

19.   In which school did Fives originate?   **Eton**

20.   Ryeland, Kerry Hill and Roscommon are all breeds
      of which animal?   **Sheep**

Round 65

1.   What word was used for the eastern end of the
      Mediterranean and the adjoining countries?   **Levant**

2.   Who chaired *Have I Got News For You?* and acted
      in *One Foot In the Grave*?   **Angus Deayton**

3.   In Genesis, which land was said to lie to the east of
      Eden?   **Nod**

4.   Maximilian was installed as emperor of which
      country by Napoleon III?   **Mexico**

5.   What is a phalarope? Is it a bird, a microbe or a
      formation of troops?   **A bird**

6.   True or false: the first US Open Golf Championship
      was played on a 9 hole course?   **True**

7.   On which island was the maze containing the
      Minotaur?   **Crete**

8.   By what name was Mohammed Ahmed, the man
      who took Khartoum in 1885, known?   **The Mahdi**

9.   What name is given to a person or thing that brings
      bad luck?   **Jinx or Jonah**

10.   What does a gamophobe fear?   **Marriage**

11.   A slave, Toussaint L'Overture, led a revolt of black
      slaves which overthrew the government of which
      country in 1791?   **Haiti**

12. In mythology, what happened if you drank the water of the River Lethe?   **You forgot**

13. Who played Blott in the TV serial *Blott On The Landscape*?   **David Suchet**

14. Under what guise does Caroline Hook appear on television?   **Mrs Merton**

15. What binding medium is used in gouache painting? Is it egg white, egg yolk or glue?   **Glue**

16. Exactly where is your coccyx?   **Base of spine**

17. Which character has been played in films by, among others, Frank Langella, Jack Palance, Gary Oldman and Francis Lederer?   **Dracula**

18. Who had a No 1 hit in 1982 with *Happy Talk*?   **Captain Sensible**

19. What are Ashvine Challenger, Old Hooky, White Boar and Hard Tackle?   **Real ales**

20. Which metal is extracted from Sphalerite?   **Zinc**

Round 66

1. Which food was miraculously supplied to the Israelites in the wilderness?   **Manna**

2. True or false: prosthetics is the science of creating and fitting artificial limbs?   **True**

3. Who had a 1986 No 1 with *The Lady in Red*?   **Chris de Burgh**

4. Complete this nautical trio: the *Pinta*, the *Nina* and the . . . . . . (what)?   *Santa Maria*

5.   What is the opposite of 'dunce'?   **Dux**

6.   Who succeeded Anthony Eden as Prime Minister?   **Harold Macmillan**

7.   A leopard's head, an anchor, a castle and a harp are all used as what?   **Hallmarks**

8.   Who is the first female in the order of accession to the British throne?   **Princess Beatrice**

9.   In the Bible, who was sent into the Land of Nod as a punishment?   **Cain**

10. Who wrote the novel *The History of Pendennis*?   **William M Thackeray**

11. Which one word means to cultivate, up to the time of and a money drawer?   **Till**

12. Who was the first team to win the FA Cup at Wembley?   **Bolton Wanderers**

13. Who led the bank robbers in the film *The League of Gentlemen*?   **Jack Hawkins**

14. Which poem begins famously with the lines "I leant upon a coppice gate / When Frost was spectre-gray"?   ***The Darkling Thrush***

15. Which Gilbert and Sullivan operetta has the subtitle *The King of Barataria*?   ***The Gondoliers***

16. Who said, after winning the Grand National: "Sex is an anti-climax after that"?   **Mick Fitzgerald**

17. What is the capital of New York state?   **Albany**

18. True or false: SOS is not an abbreviation for Save Our Souls?   **True**

19.   What name is given to the stiffening of the body
      after death?   **Rigor mortis**

20.   In what year were dog licences abolished?   **1988**

Round 67

1.   In what year did Queen Victoria die?   **1901**

2.   Who played Isadora Duncan in the film *Isadora*?
                                        Vanessa Redgrave

3.   In which Italian city can you see Juliet's house and
      balcony? Is it Genoa, Bologna or Verona?   **Verona**

4.   Whose life is dealt with in the novel *The Big
      Fisherman*?   **Simon (St) Peter's**

5.   By what name was writer Mary Westmacott better
      known?   **Agatha Christie**

6.   Which song contains these lines: "People come to
      their windows. They all stare at me. Shake their
      heads in sorrow, saying 'Who can that fool be?' "?
                                        Walking in the Rain

7.   What nationality was World Motor Racing
      Champion Juan Fangio?   **Argentinian**

8.   Apart from a dance, what is a bolero?   **Short jacket**

9.   Which artist's biography was entitled *The Fake's
      Progress*?   **Tom Keating's**

10.   Who created Noggin the Nog, Bagpuss and The
      Clangers?   **Oliver Postgate**

11.   In which African country was the series *The Flame
      Trees of Thika* set?   **Kenya**

12. Who had Top Ten hits with *Body Talk*, *Just an Illusion* and *Music and Lights*?   **Imagination**

13. Who launched the Zike (electric bike) in 1992?   **Clive Sinclair**

14. True or false: the Bible says Delilah cut off Samson's hair?   **False (She had a man do it.)**

15. Who in 1992 broke Pat Eddery's run of four consecutive Flat Jockey Championships?   **Michael Roberts**

16. Who designed the fighter bomber the Mosquito?   **De Havilland**

17. Who played Officer Barraclough in *Porridge*?   **Brian Wilde**

18. Who, in a song, was thrown out 'with nothing but a fine tooth comb'?   **Bill Bailey**

19. What is a half hunter?   **A pocket watch**

20. What are the grades of proficiency in judo called?   **Dans**

Round 68

1. If you were described as an ectomorph, would you be fat, thin, tall, short or pale?   **Thin**

2. In which sport could you have a York Round and a Hereford Round?   **Archery**

3. What is champaign?   **Flat, open country**

4. Is a brumby a wild horse, a thorny bush or a standing stone?   **A wild horse**

5. What is the chemical symbol for arsenic? **As**

6. Which Canadian province is named after one of Queen Victoria's daughters? **Alberta**

7. What was the first country to use number plates on its road vehicles? Was it Britain, the USA or France? **France**

8. Whose Top Ten hits included *Let Me In*, *The Proud One* and *Going Home*? **The Osmonds**

9. True or false: Gustav Holst called Neptune *The Bringer of War*? **False (*The Mystic*)**

10. Which Welsh bay lies between St Govan's Head and Worms Head? **Camarthen Bay**

11. To what does the old saying 'Dog goes, cat comes' refer? **The waxing and waning of the moon**

12. Who got to No 3 with *Joe le Taxi*? **Vanessa Paradis**

13. What is the Scottish word for a rough cottage or hut where farm workers lived? **Bothy**

14. What successful British film followed the lives of a group of male strippers? ***The Full Monty***

15. What would you be doing if you practised banting: yachting, dieting or crochet? **Dieting**

16. Which of D H Lawrence's novels is set in Australia? ***Kangaroo***

17. What was the Derby Scheme of 1915? Was it conscription, dole or food vouchers? **Conscription**

18. Who played the lead in the films *The Joker is Wild*, *A Hole in the Head* and *Never So Few*? **Frank Sinatra**

19. Which country was formerly called Dutch East Indies? **Indonesia**

20. Which one word means fill with water and sink, an originator and a person who casts metal? **Founder**

Round 69

1. In *Rising Damp* which character was the son of an African tribal chief? **Philip**

2. Which Berkshire school did Prince Charles attend? **Cheam**

3. Timbrology was an old name for bell-ringing, tree felling or stamp collecting? Which? **Stamp collecting**

4. What did Mark Twain describe as "a cabbage with a college education"? **Cauliflower**

5. True or false: Pearl Buck was the first woman to win the Nobel prize for Literature? **False**

6. Who was known as the Widow at Windsor? **Queen Victoria**

7. What was Winston Churchill's home in Kent called? **Chartwell**

8. What was the ancient name of Iraq? **Mesopotamia**

9. Of which modern instrument was the sackbut a forerunner? **Trombone**

10. In the drink 'Gin and It' what is 'It'? **Italian Vermouth**

11. Who played the headmaster in the TV series *Whack-O*? **Jimmy Edwards**

12. Whose musical works were catalogued by Kochel numbers? **Mozart's**

13. Who played the female lead to Rock Hudson in *Magnificent Obsession*? **Jane Wyman**

14. In the Bible, who was the father of Enoch? **Cain**

15. What does 'sub.rosa' mean? **In secret**

16. Which was the only No 1 for the Dave Clark Five? ***Glad All Over***

17. Which fish is known as Fish Royal? **Sturgeon**

18. Manganese Bronze Holdings are the makers of which famous vehicle? **Black taxis**

19. *Dwt.* was an abbreviation for what? **Pennyweight**

20. Which sport was played by Peanut Louie? **Lawn Tennis**

Round 70

1. True or false: a Turk's Head is a type of knot? **True**

2. How old is a quadragenarian? **40**

3. Proverbially, when is the darkest hour? **Before the dawn**

4. In which county is the resort of Budleigh Salterton? **Devon**

5. In our language from 1957, what is the Russian for 'travelling companion'? **Sputnik**

6. Which bird was once known as the halcyon? **Kingfisher**

7.   What was hokey-pokey, sold on the streets until the 1920s? Was it ice-cream, toffee or dried fish?

Ice-cream

8.   Who starred in *Death in Venice, The Damned* and *The Servant*?   **Dirk Bogarde**

9.   Which TV presenter said: "There was life before *Coronation Street*, but it didn't add up to much."?

Russell Harty

10.   Which puppet on TV was operated by Ivan Owen?

Basil Brush

11.   What would you do with spelding: solder, weave cloth or eat it?   **Eat it (Fish)**

12.   The book *Enemy Coast Ahead* was made into which famous film?   *The Dambusters*

13.   Which of these is a diamond: Star of Bethlehem, Star of India or Star of South Africa?   **Star of South Africa**

14.   Who sang with Elton John on *Act of War*?   **Millie Jackson**

15.   Which flower is the badge of the Boy Scouts?

Fleur de Lis

16.   How far south did Bonnie Prince Charlie get in 1745?   **To Derby**

17.   True or false: the poet A E Housman is associated with Cornwall?   **False (Shropshire)**

18.   Whose early films included *The Song of Bernadette* and *Laura* before he made *House of Wax*?   **Vincent Price**

19.   On which river does Leicester stand?   **River Soar**

20. Who, in 1967, became Britain's first Minister for the Arts?   **Jennie Lee**

Round 71

1.   Which song begins: "When you left me all alone, at the record hop; told me you were going out for a soda pop"?   ***Lipstick On Your Collar***

2.   How long would you have been married if you were celebrating a Platinum Anniversary?   **70 years**

3.   Where are the Highland Games held?   **Braemar**

4.   What happened near Cheddington in Buckinghamshire on 7th August, 1963?   **Great Train Robbery**

5.   Which country was ruled by King Gustavus Adolphus, the Lion of the North, in the 17th century?   **Sweden**

6.   Who wrote *The Aspern Papers*, *The Ambassadors* and *The Golden Bowl*?   **Henry James**

7.   Who wrote the plays *The Glass Menagerie* and *Cat On a Hot Tin Roof*?   **Tennessee Williams**

8.   Who played the rich rock star in the TV series *Roll Over, Beethoven*?   **Nigel Planer**

9.   Who succeeded Bob Paisley as manager of Liverpool Football Club?   **Joe Fagan**

10. Who defected to Russia with Guy Burgess in 1951?
                                        Donald MacLean

11. Of which soldier did Tennyson write: "This earth has borne no simpler, nobler, man"? Was it Wellington, Marlborough or Gordon?   **Gordon**

12. Who had Top Twenty hits with *I Feel Free*, *Strange Brew* and *Badge*?   **Cream**

13. The mastiff and the greyhound were crossed to produce which breed of dog?   **Great Dane**

14. Who directed the film *Bird*, the film biography of Charlie Parker?   **Clint Eastwood**

15. What is the capital of the Orkneys?   **Kirkwall**

16. True or false: Eddie Shah's 1986 newspaper was *Today*?   **True**

17. What was the middle name of the writer William Thackeray?   **Makepeace**

18. Where do bees carry the pollen they collect?   **On their back legs (in a 'basket')**

19. Osbert, Sacheverell and Edith . . . . What is the surname?   **Sitwell**

20. For what did Madame Helen Blavatsky achieve fame?   **Spiritualism**

Round 72

1. On TV, who played *The Man From Atlantis*?   **Patrick Duffy**

2. What pseudonym was used by Aurore Dupin, mistress of Chopin?   **George Sand**

3. To what did the Spastics Society change its name in the 1990s? Was it Assist, Care or Scope?   **Scope**

4. For what product is the island of Murano, off
    Venice, famous?   **Glass**

5. There were five Roman Emperors in 68-69 AD.
    Galba, Otho and Vitellius were three of them; name
    one of the other two.   **Nero or Vespasian**

6. Which word means the knack of making lucky
    discoveries by accident?   **Serendipity**

7. Which part of your body would suffer from
    trichosis?   **The hair**

8. Who played Major Harry Truscott in the TV series
    Fairly Secret Army?   **Geoffrey Palmer**

9. Who wrote the novels *Pied Piper*, *No Highway* and
    A Town Like Alice?   **Nevil Shute**

10. Who had Top Ten hits with *Woman in Love*, *My
    Simple Heart* and *Take Good Care of Yourself*?
                                           Three Degrees

11. Which political party's HQ is at 150 Walworth
    Road in London?   **Labour Party**

12. True or false: Prince Charles is the Earl of
    Inverness?   **False (It is Prince Andrew.)**

13. What name is given to Buddhist shrines built in the
    form of a tower?   **Pagodas**

14. What is the popular name for the antirrhinum?
                                             Snapdragon

15. Which word, used in proof reading, means 'Leave
    as printed' or 'Let it stand'?   **Stet**

16. Who played a female undertaker in the TV series *In
    Loving Memory*?   **Thora Hird**

17.   In the Tarzan novels, who was known as Korak?

Tarzan's son

18.   Why should flags be flown on Government buildings on February 6th?   **Anniversary of the Queen's accession**

19.   Who headed the committee investigating 'sleaze' in public life in 1995?   **Lord Nolan**

20.   What is a titi? Is it a small crocodile, a tropical songbird or a monkey?   **A monkey**

Round 73

1.   Who played the title role in the comedy film *The Missionary*?   **Michael Palin**

2.   Who was the mother-in-law of Angus Ogilvy?

Princess Marina

3.   Who wrote *Puck of Pook's Hill* and *Rewards and Fairies*?   **Rudyard Kipling**

4.   What sort of weapon was an arbalest? Was it a musket, a mace or a crossbow?   **A crossbow**

5.   Which frigate was launched secretly in 1986 in Wallsend to replace a ship lost in the Falklands?

HMS *Coventry*

6.   Who had Top Ten hits with *Best Years of Our Lives*, *High Life* and *Ay Ay Ay Ay Moosey*?

Modern Romance

7.   Of whom did Dennis Healey say that being attacked by him was like being savaged by a dead sheep?   **Geoffrey Howe**

8. True or false: the Thames is the longest river wholly in England? **True**

9. What is the capital of Manitoba province in Canada? **Winnipeg**

10. In which county is the Parliamentary constituency of South Hams? **Devon**

11. Who was banned for two one-day cricket internationals in 1986 after admitting he'd smoked cannabis? **Ian Botham**

12. Which domestic pet is descended from the cavy? **Guinea-pig**

13. Who wrote *A Farewell To Arms* and *Death in the Afternoon*? **Ernest Hemingway**

14. Which TV series featured the character Boss Hogg? ***The Dukes of Hazzard***

15. In the nursery rhyme *Cock A Doodle Doo*, what has my master lost? **His fiddling stick**

16. What name is given to ornamental gilded bronze, used to decorate furniture? **Ormolu**

17. What was the name of Don Lang's backing group? **The Frantic Five**

18. As what did Walt Whitman make his name? **A poet**

19. What was the title of the modern film version of *Cyrano de Bergerac* starring Steve Martin as a fire chief? ***Roxanne***

20. In which country was the military Tet Offensive launched in 1968? **South Vietnam**

Round 74

1. Which part of the body is affected by Crohn's Disease?   **Intestines**

2. Whose catchphrase was "Shut that door."?   **Larry Grayson**

3. In which US town is the Rose Bowl, venue for the post season football game between college champions?   **Pasadena**

4. True or false: Harry Houdini was born in Budapest?   **True**

5. Where was "the shot heard all around the world" fired?   **Sarajevo**

6. What nationality was Canute, King of England from 1016 to 1035?   **Danish**

7. What sort of garment was a Sloppy Joe?   **A loose sweater**

8. Which famous radio programme ended with the words "Carry on, London"?   ***In Town Tonight***

9. Which palace was given to the Duke of Marlborough as a reward for military services?   **Blenheim**

10. J McGill, A Long and T Watson all won British championships in which of the following: marbles, draughts or quoits?   **Draughts**

11. Who played Don Quixote in the film *Man of La Mancha*?   **Peter O'Toole**

12. Whose Top Ten hits included *Oh Well*, *Man of the World* and *Tusk*?   **Fleetwood Mac**

13. Which musical TV series was described as "sheer filth, obnoxious and bordering on pornography" when first broadcast in 1978? **Pennies From Heaven**

14. In what field was the Bauhaus movement? **Architecture**

15. What was the title of the famous folklore study by Sir J G Frazer? **The Golden Bough**

16. The Whittaker system divides the living world into how many kingdoms? Is it 5, 7 or 12? **5**

17. What was silent film star Fatty Arbuckle's Christian name? **Roscoe**

18. What was the name of the spiv played by James Beck in *Dad's Army*? **Walker**

19. Desmond, Taiwan, Douglas and Pattie are all slang words for what? **Academic Degrees**

20. True or false: the German U-Boat U-65, launched in 1916, was said to be haunted? **True**

Round 75

1. Which rat trained the Teenage Mutant Ninja Turtles? **Splinter**

2. Which element is last alphabetically? **Zirconium**

3. *The Flowers o' the Forest* is a traditional lament for Scots who fell where? **Flodden**

4. Who said: "Don't point that beard at me: it might go off."? **Groucho Marx**

5. In the poem *Beowulf*, how does Beowulf die? **Killed by a dragon**

6. What is the administrative HQ of Shropshire?
Shrewsbury

7. Ben Webster, Lester Young and Steve Lacy are all associated with which instrument? **Saxophone**

8. Who published the book *Missionary Travels in South Africa* in 1857? **David Livingstone**

9. Which British city contains the Jew's House, the Usher Gallery and the National Cycle Museum?
Lincoln

10. Under what pseudonym did Sir William Connor write in *The Daily Mirror*? **Cassandra**

11. Who was the subject of the Mel Brooks' film subtitled *Men in Tights*? **Robin Hood**

12. From where does Cathay Pacific Airways come?
Hong Kong

13. Eric Idle and Neil Innes sent up the Beatles by forming which group on TV? **The Rutles**

14. Which Elvis film was based on the play *A Stone For Danny Fisher*? *King Creole*

15. Which US union, formerly led by Jimmy Hoffa, was at one time the largest in the USA? **Teamsters**

16. True or false: the 'Pilot' in the famous Punch cartoon *Dropping the Pilot* refers to Bismarck? **True**

17. Which sport might involve a schuss? **Skiing**

18. In Greek mythology, what did the gods eat?
Ambrosia

19. Who had Top Ten hits with *I Can't Explain*, *Happy Jack* and *Pictures of Lily*?   **The Who**

20. What relationship was William the Conqueror to King Stephen?   **Grandfather**

Round 76

1. Which Brontë sister wrote *Shirley*?   **Charlotte**

2. What does the expression "The old woman is plucking her goose" mean?   **It's snowing**

3. Where are your zygomatic, ethmoid and vomer bones?   **In the skull**

4. What was the setting for the 1987 film *Gardens of Stone*?   **Arlington National Cemetery**

5. Which country beat France to win the 1999 Davis Cup Final?   **Australia**

6. What is a young kangaroo called?   **A Joey**

7. Nobles, unites, bezants and angels were all what?   **Coins**

8. Where on a ship would you find the lubber's hole?   **On the mast**

9. What was the title of the 1966 TV series about a cockney charlady, played by Kathleen Harrison, who inherited an industrial empire?   *Mrs Thursday*

10. The character 'Old Mortality' devoted his life to doing what? Was it planting fruit trees, cleaning and restoring tombstones or burying paupers?   **Cleaning and restoring tombstones**

11. What is a bissextile year?   **A leap year**

12. True or false: there is a country called the Federated
    States of Micronesia?   **True**

13. What must when the Devil drives?   **Needs**

14. Which English king was nicknamed The Merry
    Monarch?   **Charles II**

15. Before Frank Spencer, "Some mothers do 'ave 'em"
    was a catchphrase in whose comedy radio
    programme?   **Jimmy Clitheroe's**

16. Who played the other half of *The Odd Couple* when
    Tony Randall played Felix?   **Jack Klugman**

17. In Norse mythology, which maidens conduct fallen
    heroes to Valhalla?   **The Valkyries**

18. To what did Pussyfoot Johnson devote his energy?
    Was it legalising brothels, temperance, or a
    detective agency?   **Temperance**

19. What is a Miller's Thumb? Is it a type of bean, a fish
    or a tallow candle?   **Fish (Bullhead)**

20. Where did 'expects' replace 'confides' to save the
    number of flags?   **Trafalgar**
                          (In Nelson's famous signal.)

Round 77

1. Who had Top Ten hits with *The Cutter* and *The
   Killing Moon*?   **Echo and the Bunnymen**

2. Who wrote the plays *The Cocktail Party* and *The
   Family Reunion*?   **T S Eliot**

3. What was the name of Kaiser Bill's mother?
    Victoria

4. Who played Malcolm X in the 1992 film of that
    name?   **Denzel Washington**

5. Olympia is the capital of which US state?
    Washington

6. Which Sheridan play features Sir Lucius O'Trigger
    and Anthony Absolute?   *The Rivals*

7. By what name was Agnes Gonxha Bejaxhui better
    known?   **Mother Teresa**

8. True or false: the first Porsche was a sports version
    of the Volkswagen Beetle?   **True**

9. In which city is Suffolk's administrative HQ?
    Ipswich

10. For what was Gerardus Mercator famous?   **Maps
    of the earth**

11. Who had No 1 hits with *I Love You* and *The Minute
    You're Gone*?   **Cliff Richard**

12. Which one word means a loud noise, an account of a
    speech and a statement of a pupil's work?   **Report**

13. In a 1995 survey, which capital was rated Europe's
    cleanest? Was it London, Athens or Paris?   **London**

14. Which of the Shetland Isles is regarded as Britain's
    most remote island?   **Foula**

15. What was the name of George Stephenson's first
    locomotive?   *Blucher*

16.   In which English county is the Wyre Forest?
      Worcestershire

17.   Which game birds' group name is a tok?
      Capercaillie

18.   Which of the following has the most fat content:
      bacon, almonds or Cheddar cheese?   **Almonds**

19.   Which Briton broke the world land speed record at
      Daytona in 1927 and 1929?   **Henry Segrave**

20.   Who played the monster in the film *Young
      Frankenstein*?   **Peter Boyle**

Round 78

1.   Which woodwind instrument is also called the
      octave flute?   **Piccolo**

2.   What nickname was given in World War 2 to
      scientists or backroom boys?   **Boffins**

3.   In which sport would you use the term
      'flanconnade'?   **Fencing**

4.   True or false: John Dryden was the first Poet
      Laureate?   **True**

5.   What is supernaculum? Is it fine wine, part of a
      building or part of a horse's harness?   **Fine wine**

6.   Which country lies between Algeria and Libya?
      Tunisia

7.   Which TV show produced the catch phrases "Sock
      it to me", "Here come de Judge" and "Very
      interesting – but stupid"?   ***Rowan and Martin's
      Laugh-In***

8. Which actress was Oscar nominated for *Silkwood*
    and won an Oscar for *Moonstruck*?   **Cher**

9. Who are members of the Q Guild?   **Butchers**

10. For what is Chinge Hall in Lancashire famous?
                                              It's haunted

11. Where was the first tennis club founded in England?
    Was it Leamington Spa, Wimbledon or Bath?
                                         Leamington Spa

12. William Adams, who learned to sail with Francis
    Drake, later became so respected in a foreign
    country that to this day they hold an annual festival
    in his honour. Which country? Is it Holland, Japan
    or Denmark?   **Japan**

13. Which Literary prize has been won by *Injury Time*,
    Hawksmoor and *Picture Palace*?   **Whitbread
                                                   Award**

14. Which British ship – a liner – was the first to be
    sunk by a U-Boat on the first day of World War 2?
                                               Athenia

15. Who was the last European king to be assassinated?
    Was it Alexander I of Jugoslavia, Carlos I of Spain
    or Giorgios II of Greece?   **Alexander I**

16. Whose Top Ten hits included *Johnny Come Home*
    and *Suspicious Minds*?   **Fine Young Cannibals**

17. Where exactly in your body is fibrin found?   **In the
                                                    blood**

18. If someone carried out rolfing on you, would they
    be massaging you, telling your fortune or showing
    you card tricks?   **Massaging**

19. In which country did the King of Alba rule?

Scotland

20. True or false: the first Winter Olympics took place in 1928?   **False (1924)**

Round 79

1. Who wrote *The Fourth Protocol*?   **Frederick Forsyth**

2. Which word means a dollar, a male rabbit and a back-arching jump?   **Buck**

3. Whose Top Ten hits include *How Will I Know*, *Greatest Love of All* and *So Emotional*?   **Whitney Houston**

4. Which common gas was once called azote?   **Nitrogen**

5. Whose catchphrase was "Mind my bike"?   **Jack Warner's**

6. According to Shakespeare's play, who was Prince of Tyre?   **Pericles**

7. What kind of song is a berceuse?   **Lullaby or cradle-song**

8. What is the official language of the Ivory Coast?   **French**

9. Which medal now ranks second to the Victoria Cross for bravery?   **Conspicuous Gallantry Cross**

10. Which common bird is also called the dunnock?   **Hedge Sparrow**

11. According to the nursery rhyme, what kind of cake were the fighting lion and unicorn given?   **Plum cake**

12. Which film starts with Mel Brooks and Anne Bancroft singing *Sweet Georgia Brown* in Polish? **To Be or Not To Be (1983)**

13. What was a bridewell? **A prison**

14. Who bought the Castle of Mey in 1952? **The Queen Mother**

15. Who played a delayed headmaster in the film *Clockwise*? **John Cleese**

16. True or false: Alexander the Great died at Alexandria? **False (Babylon)**

17. Who played the title role in the film *Forrest Gump*? **Tom Hanks**

18. What is a gonk? **A furry toy**

19. What is the capital of the Dominican republic? **Santo Domingo**

20. Who played the forever changing scientist in *The Incredible Hulk*? **Bill Bixby**

Round 80

1. What does an ichthyophagist do? **Eats fish**

2. Which game was invented in India in 1875 and reached England ten years later? **Snooker**

3. Is cassata a type of mortar, pasta or ice-cream? **Ice-cream**

4. In which country did Guy Gibson die? **Holland**

5. Which is the only bird in the Chinese calendar? **Rooster**

6.   Who had a No 1 hit in 1974 with *Billy Don't be a Hero*?   **Paper Lace**

7.   What is breccia? Is it a type of moss, a kind of rock or seaweed?   **Rock**

8.   Which country has the shortest coastline?   **Monaco**

9.   In which TV series did Ralph Waite play the father of a big family?   ***The Waltons***

10.   In which country was President Allende overthrown by General Pinochet?   **Chile**

11.   In which sport would you use a trudgen?   **Swimming**

12.   True or false: A wapacut is a species of eagle?   **False (It is an owl.)**

13.   In which building are the Promenade Concerts now held?   **Royal Albert Hall**

14.   Who had a No 1 hit with *China In Your Hand*?   **T'Pau**

15.   According to tradition, Bonnie Prince Charlie gave Captain McKinnon the recipe for which liqueur?   **Drambuie**

16.   Which postal item was copyrighted by J P Charlton in 1861?   **Postcard**

17.   Which religious movement, founded in 1872, was originally called the International Bible Students?   **Jehovah's Witnesses**

18.   In sport, which game has the largest playing pitch?   **Polo**

19. Which song, popular with both sides in World War 2, was written by Hans Leip, a German soldier in World War 1? **Lili Marlene**

20. The Kit-Cat Club, founded in London in 1700, took its name from something that was served there. Was it mutton pies, chocolate cake or iced coffee? **Mutton Pies**

Round 81

1. What fires a SLBM? **Submarine**

2. The Hapsburgs, the Austrian Royal family, were renowned for a certain physical characteristic. What was it? **The lip (or lower jaw)**

3. In physics, for what is Hare's apparatus used? **To compare or find densities of liquids**

4. Who would carry out bosing: a brewer, an archaeologist or a sign painter? **Archaeologist**

5. Michael Ostrog, Kosminski, M J Druitt and J K Stephen were all suspected of being whom? **Jack the Ripper**

6. Who wrote the poems *Locksley Hall*, *Maud* and *The Idylls of the King*? **Tennyson**

7. What is the capital of Colombia? **Bogota**

8. True or false: Indian Ink originally came from China? **True**

9. To an Australian, what are strides? **Trousers**

10. In equestrianism, which event tests the horse's obedience? **Dressage**

11. Which of the *Road To* films was set in the Klondike Gold Rush?   ***Road To Utopia***

12. What was originally known as the Pari Mutuel?   **The Tote**

13. What does the Trachtenberg System involve?   **Mathematical calculations**

14. Which European city is known as *The Bride of the Sea*?   **Venice**

15. What is matze? Is it Jewish bread, Japanese fishcakes or Polish sausage?   **Jewish bread**

16. Which flower was nicknamed 'Kiss-behind-the-garden-gate'?   **Pansy**

17. Who had Top Ten hits with *Heaven Must be Missing an Angel* and *Whodunnit*?   **Tavares**

18. In America, what is a cayuse?   **A horse**

19. Who presented the TV gameshow *Midas Touch*?   **Bradley Walsh**

20. What shape is the body of a balalaika?   **Triangular**

Round 82

1. Which actor produced the Whitehall farces in the1950s and 1960s?   **Brian Rix**

2. Who said: "I'm sure I was wrong on a number of occasions, but I can't think of anything immediately."?   **Margaret Thatcher**

3. For what is bhp the abbreviation?   **Brake horse power**

4. In poetry, who roams the Gromboolian plain looking for his Jumbly Girl with the sky blue hands? **The Dong (with the luminous nose)**

5. Who presents the TV programme *You've Been Framed*? **Jeremy Beadle**

6. Who played the title role in the film *The Elephant Man*? **John Hurt**

7. Which was the only full-scale naval battle of World War 1? **Jutland**

8. With what was Morton's Fork concerned? Was it road-building, taxation or gardening? **Taxation**

9. Where is the HQ of the World Health Organisation? **Geneva**

10. Who wrote *Lords and Ladies* and *Small Gods*? **Terry Pratchett**

11. Fermin Cacho won the 1992 Olympic 1500 metres. Give his nationality. **Spanish**

12. In the TV series *Telford's Change*, what was Telford's job? **Bank manager**

13. When the witches chased Tam O'Shanter, what did they get? **His horse's tail**

14. Rococo and Baroque are styles of what? **Architecture**

15. Who had Top Ten hits with *Me the Peaceful Heart*, *Leave a Little Love* and *The Man Who Sold the World*? **Lulu**

16. Who are in charge in a theocracy? **Priests**

17. Which sea is connected to the Baltic Sea by the Kiel Canal? **North Sea**

18. What would happen if you took an emetic medicine? **You'd vomit**

19. Which Prime Minister was the Earl of Chatham? **William Pitt**

20. True or false: *The Modern Prometheus* was the subtitle of the novel *Dracula*? **False (It was the subtitle of *Frankenstein*.)**

Round 83

1. Proverbially, what do late workers burn? **The midnight oil**

2. Which day follows Shrove Tuesday? **Ash Wednesday**

3. Under which name was Luke McMasters a professional wrestler? **Giant Haystacks**

4. A 3,000 year old bas-relief was sold for $11 million in 1994. Where had it been for many years: in a cow shed, a school tuckshop or a garden? **School Tuckshop**

5. Who wrote *Moon River*? **Henry Mancini**

6. Which puppet series sprang out of *Sesame Street*? **The Muppet Show**

7. Experiments to prove the earth was flat or otherwise were carried out in 1838 and 1870 at the Old Bedford Level. What was the Old Bedford Level? **A canal**

8. In the sci-fi film *Them*, what were 'them'? **Giant ants**

9. Who would have practised his skill on a quintain? **A (Mounted) Knight**

10. In which sport are there events called The Hambletonian and Little Brown Jug? **Harness Racing**

11. Who are thespians? **Actors**

12. Who had a No 1 with *Doctorin' the Tardis*? **Timelords**

13. Who wrote *The Scorpio Illusion* and *The Road To Omaha*? **Robert Ludlum**

14. Give the name of Alistair Cooke's long-running weekly radio talk on the BBC. ***Letter From America***

15. With which sport is Clare Francis associated? **Sailing**

16. True or false: Laurence Sterne created a character called Tristram Shandy? **True**

17. What was the name of Queen Victoria's residence on the Isle of Wight? **Osborne House**

18. What kind of fish is a hammerhead? **Shark**

19. Who wears a chasuble? Is it a priest, a knight in armour or a diver? **A priest**

20. David Duckham, Mervyn Davies and Tony Ward were all voted Player of the Year in the 1970s in which sport? **Rugby**

Round 84

1. Which school film had the theme music *Rock Around the Clock*?   **Blackboard Jungle**

2. In which profession was Nelson Mandela qualified?   **Legal (Lawyer)**

3. Who came second when Ronald Reagan was first elected US president?   **Jimmy Carter**

4. Who played the lead – a canal lock-keeper – in the TV series *The River*?   **David Essex**

5. In which county is Skegness?   **Lincolnshire**

6. Who wrote *Rodney Stone*, *The White Company* and *The Lost World*?   **Sir Arthur Conan Doyle**

7. Who was Prime Minister when the First World War started?   **Herbert Asquith**

8. Traditionally, the word 'lascar' was used to describe Indians doing what job?   **Sailors**

9. Which religious order was founded by Ignatius Loyola?   **Jesuits**

10. Which product was advertised on TV by Sharon Maughan and Anthony Head?   **Gold Blend Coffee**

11. In which book of the Bible is the story of Samson? Is it Deuteronomy, Joshua or Judges?   **Judges**

12. True or false: bonny-clabber is a type of cloth?   **False (It is a drink.)**

13. Who played Conan in the films *Conan the Barbarian* and *Conan the Destroyer*?   **Arnold Schwarzenegger**

14. Which Prime Minister resigned as a result of the
    Suez crisis?   **Anthony Eden**

15. What exactly is a chow-chow?   **A dog**

16. Opium, Californian and Yellow Horned are all
    varieties of which flower?   **Poppy**

17. Which Frenchwoman won the Wimbledon Ladies
    Singles five times in succession in the 1920s?
                                          Suzanne Lenglen

18. Which river is known as the King of Waters?
                                                 Amazon

19. Who composed the orchestral suites *London*, *London
    Again* and *From Meadow to Mayfair*?   **Eric Coates**

20. Who is the Queen's representative in each county?
                                         Lord Lieutenant

Round 85

1. Devil's Tower in Wyoming played an important
   part in which 1977 film?   *Close Encounters of the
                                           Third Kind*

2. Which one word means a unit of weight, an
   enclosure for animals and to beat?   **Pound**

3. What was the nickname of actress Emily Charlotte
   Langtry?   **Jersey Lily**

4. Which is the main trophy for eights won at Henley
   Royal Regatta?   **Grand Challenge Cup**

5. Which Shakespearean character said: "I'll put a
   girdle round about the earth in forty minutes."?
                                                   Puck

6. Who was the dizzy blonde who couldn't add up in the TV show *The Golden Shot*?   **Anne Aston**

7. What was a Spanish worm: a hidden nail, a weevil in ship's biscuits or a poisonous snake?   **A hidden nail**

8. True or false: Scott Joplin was the originator of boogie woogie?   **False (He was famous for ragtime.)**

9. What is a tench?   **A fish**

10. Which is the largest of these islands: Zanzibar, Sri Lanka or Madagascar?   **Madagascar**

11. Which game includes Mr Bun the Baker, his wife and children?   **Happy Families**

12. Who played the male lead in Hitchcock's *Marnie*?   **Sean Connery**

13. Which song, written by The Corries, has replaced *Scotland the Brave* as the unofficial Scottish national anthem at football and rugby matches?   ***Flower of Scotland***

14. What cried out to warn the giant when it was stolen by Jack before he escaped down the beanstalk?   **The Harp**

15. Which strip cartoon was drawn by Trog?   ***Flook***

16. Name the Duke of Bedford's stately home.   **Woburn Abbey**

17. What was the name of the woman in John Cleland's book *Memoirs of a Woman of Pleasure*?   **Fanny Hill**

18. Who were the German husband and wife team who popularised underwater TV programmes in the 1950s and 1960s?   **Hans and Lottie Hass**

19. Which unit of measurement was based on the
    distance from the elbow to the tip of the middle
    finger?   **Cubit**

20. Anything 'napiform' is shaped like which
    vegetable?   **Turnip**

Round 86

1. Which newspaper's headline on 4th May 1982 was
   "Gotcha!"?   ***The Sun's***

2. Which restaurant guide was launched by Raymond
   Postgate in 1949?   ***Good Food Guide***

3. Five countries provided most of the UN troops in
   Korea in the 1950s. USA, Britain and Australia
   were three; name one of the other two.   **Canada or
                                                       Turkey**

4. Where is the Ideal Home Exhibition held?   **Earl's
                                                        Court**

5. Who had a No1 hit in 1988 with *Heaven Is a Place
   On Earth*?   **Belinda Carlisle**

6. Who played Richard Hannay in the Hitchcock
   version of *The 39 Steps*?   **Robert Donat**

7. What kind of creature was Robert Louis
   Stevenson's Modestine?   **A donkey**

8. Which planes were used by the Dam Busters?
                                                     Lancasters

9. In which sport did the Russian, Prince Oblensky,
   represent England?   **Rugby Union**

10. What honorary title is given to the MP who has sat in the Commons for the longest uninterrupted period?   **Father of the House**

11. Who played Apollo Creed in the *Rocky* movies?
                                          Carl Weathers

12. On TV, who played The Singing Detective?
                                          Michael Gambon

13. Which African country's capital is named after an American President?   **Liberia**

14. What is the name of the wise baboon in *The Lion King*?   **Rafiki**

15. Who founded the magazine *Time* and the pictorial weekly *Life*?   **Henry Robinson Luce**

16. Which member of the Royal family married Marina of Greece in 1934?   **Duke of Kent**

17. Who played Leslie Grantham's brother, a priest, in *The Paradise Club*?   **Don Henderson**

18. Which county won the Cricket County Championship seven times in succession in the 1950s?   **Surrey**

19. Which Commonwealth country has the ringgit as its unit of currency?   **Malaysia**

20. Who won a gold medal for Britain in the 1960 Olympics for the 50 kilometre walk?   **Don Thompson**

Round 87

1. In which English county was willow-pattern china created?   **Staffordshire**

2.   What would you keep in a cresset: flowers, fire, jewels or guns?   **Fire**

3.   Which vegetable is in the dish Egg Florentine?   **Spinach**

4.   In which sport is there a bonspiel?   **Curling**

5.   Which London theatre boasted "We never closed."?   **Windmill**

6.   Who sings the title song for the TV series *One Foot in the Grave*?   **Eric Idle**

7.   Which was the first major German city to be captured by the Allies in World War 2?   **Aachen**

8.   From which country do Moselle wines come?   **Germany**

9.   Which country's national anthem is called *The Peaceful Banks of the River Ipiranga*?   **Brazil's**

10.   What is a 'cryptogam'? Is it a code, a marine animal, a plant or an ancient monument?   **A plant**

11.   Who wrote *Joseph Andrews*, *Jonathan Wild* and *Tom Jones*?   **Henry Fielding**

12.   The French call it Lac Leman, the Germans Genfersee. What do we call it?   **Lake Geneva**

13.   Which former European country was ruled by the Hohenzollerns?   **Prussia**

14.   From which animal did Jenner develop his smallpox vaccine?   **Cow**

15.   Who was appointed head of the Spanish Inquisition in 1483?   **Torquemada**

16. What is a mature horse below the height of fourteen and a half hands called? **A pony**

17. Who had Top Ten hits in the 1970s with *All Right Now*, *My Brother Jake* and *Wishing Well*? **Free**

18. From which language does the word 'ketchup' come? **Chinese**

19. Who composed the music for *A Fistful of Dollars*, *For a Few Dollars More* and *The Good, the Bad and the Ugly*? **Ennio Morricone**

20. In which country is November 2nd a National Holiday, celebrated as 'Day of the Dead'? **Mexico**

Round 88

1. Which actor played Mr Allison in *Heaven Knows, Mr Allison*? **Robert Mitchum**

2. On the stress scale which rates highest: pregnancy, mortgage, moving home or retirement? **Retirement**

3. Which Oscar winning song came from the film *The Thomas Crown Affair*? **Windmills of Your Mind**

4. Which Spanish painter painted the picture known as *The Rokeby Venus*? **Velasquez**

5. Which ex-Northern MP made a speech in the House of Lords on his 100th birthday? **Lord Shinwell**

6. What does a colporteur sell? **Religious books and tracts**

7. Where in Britain is the Up-Helly-Aa festivity held? **Shetlands**

8.   True or false: the bandicoot is a marsupial?   **True**

9.   Where in London is the Jerusalem Chamber?
Westminster Abbey

10. Which ancient Greek word meant "I have found it!"?   **Eureka**

11. How did the scientist Pierre Curie die?   **Run over by a cart**

12. The acre was originally a strip of land one furlong by one . . . (what)?   **Chain**

13. True or false: a kit was a small violin?   **True**

14. What colour light do ships display at night on the starboard side?   **Green**

15. Which fruit is the favourite of the orang-utan? Is it mango, pawpaw or durian?   **Durian**

16. Who chose Ottawa to be the capital of Canada?
Queen Victoria

17. Which part of London took its name from ornamental collars which were once made there? Was it Piccadilly, Holborn or Berkeley Square?
Piccadilly

18. What travels the 'mean free path'?   **A molecule**

19. In which city in 1819 did the Peterloo Massacre take place?   **Manchester**

20. Who wrote the operettas *Rose Marie* and *The Vagabond King*?   **Rudolf Friml**

Round 89

1. Which of these is NOT a lizard: chuckwalla, slowworm, gelada, agama?   **Gelada (monkey)**

2. 'Izzard' is an old word for which letter of the alphabet?   **Z**

3. In craps, if you throw a total of four, what should you throw next to win?   **4**

4. What is the popular name for the painful spasmodic contraction of a muscle?   **Cramp**

5. What was the nickname of the folk and blues singer Huddie Leadbetter?   **Leadbelly**

6. Who had a No 1 hit in 1981 with *Don't You Want Me*?   **Human League**

7. What would you drink in the cha-no-yu?   **Tea (Tea ceremony)**

8. Complete this quintet: Manhattan, Brooklyn, Bronx, Richmond and . . .   **Queens**

9. Which one word means a couple, to bind or tie close and to fill with energy?   **Brace**

10. Which famous book was compiled by Henry Baker with William Monk in 1861?   ***Hymns Ancient and Modern***

11. What name is given to metals that don't tarnish in air or water and have good resistance to acids?   **Noble**

12. On TV who played *Kavanagh QC*?   **John Thaw**

13. Which is the largest lake in Wales?   **Lake Bala**

14. Which expression for a devoted couple originates in a 1735 poem? **Darby and Joan**

15. Which international organisation was set up after World War 1 with the purpose of achieving world peace? **League of Nations**

16. In which mythology was Marduk the supreme god? **Babylonian**

17. Titania, Oberon, Miranda and Ariel are all moons of which planet? **Uranus**

18. What connects Mrs Tiggywinkle, an Arthur Lowe TV series and a wasp which builds nests of clay? **Potter**

19. In which novel does Angela Quested accuse a local doctor of rape? *A Passage To India*

20. True or false: Edward Elgar wrote the music for *Rule, Britannia!*? **False (Thomas Arne did.)**

Round 90

1. To which Biblical event does the adjective 'diluvial' refer? **The Flood**

2. Which river did Julius Caesar cross and, by doing so, cause a civil war? **Rubicon**

3. In which country did Louis Riel lead a rebellion and set up a provisional government in 1869? **Canada**

4. Who starred in the films *Monkey Business*, *Houseboat*, *Indiscreet* and *Walk, Don't Run*? **Cary Grant**

5.   Whose army spent a dreadful winter in 1777-78 at Valley Forge?   **George Washington's**

6.   In which country is Valparaiso an important port?   **Chile**

7.   In Henry III's reign, compurgation was introduced and was the forerunner of what?   **The Jury System**

8.   What is ars antiqua?   **A musical style**

9.   Who was principal conductor of the Hallé Orchestra from 1949 to 1970?   **Sir John Barbirolli**

10.   Which actress first played Miss Marple on TV in 1984?   **Joan Hickson**

11.   What colour is a giraffe's tongue?   **Blue**

12.   Which sides fought the battle of Cold Harbour?   **Union and Confederates (American Civil War)**

13.   In Greek mythology, who descended to the underworld to retrieve his wife Eurydice?   **Orpheus**

14.   Arch, whorl and loops are all parts of what?   **Fingerprints**

15.   Up to which date do we mean when the English language is referred to as 'Old English'?   **1150**

16.   Who were Patti, Maxine and Laverne?   **The Andrews Sisters**

17.   Which is the most poisonous fish in the world? Is it the pearlfish, stonefish, lionfish or needlefish?   **Stonefish**

18.   What is the chief food of baby whales?   **Their mother's milk**

19.   What is known as the Universal Solvent?   **Water**

20. Whose only Top Ten hit was *Come Softly To Me*?
Fleetwoods

Round 91

1. Sun, spectacled, brown and sloth are all species of what?
Bear

2. Bayern is the German name for which region of Germany?
Bavaria

3. What is the third name for the cougar or mountain lion?
Puma

4. In what sphere was Karsh of Ottawa famous?
Photography

5. Who played Mel Gibson's partner in the *Lethal Weapon* films?
Danny Glover

6. Of which African country was Flt Lt Jerry Rawlings leader?
Ghana

7. Which style of music is associated with the Dixie Hummingbirds, Swan Silvertones and Five Blind Boys of Alabama?
Gospel Music

8. Which British commander was so popular during the Seven Years War that many inns and pubs were named after him?
Marquis of Granby

9. Which country in 1958 introduced an economic policy called the Great Leap Forward?
China

10. With which country do you associate a guerilla group called the Tamil Tigers?
Sri Lanka

11. Who was the first jockey to win the English Derby *and* the Kentucky Derby?
Steve Cauthen

12. In ancient Greece, what was a hoplite?   **A soldier**

13. Who, in 1995, produced an album called *No Need To Argue*?   **Cranberries**

14. Who presented the TV series *Alphabet of Britain*?
Lucinda Lambton

15. Fohn, Khamsin, Brickfielder and Harmattan are all types of what?   **Winds**

16. Who said: "This is the greatest week in the history of the world since the creation."?   **Richard Nixon**

17. In which county is Jodrell Bank?   **Cheshire**

18. Whose poetry anthologies included *The North Ship*, *The Whitsun Weddings* and *High Windows*?   **Philip Larkin's**

19. Who played Dustin Hoffman's brother in the film *Marathon Man*?   **Roy Scheider**

20. For which event was the first English commemorative medal struck?   **Defeat of the Armada**

Round 92

1. What would you do in a Cambio?   **Exchange money**

2. What is a water moccasin?   **A snake**

3. Who on TV appears as Alan Partridge and Paul Calf?   **Steve Coogan**

4. Against which disease was the Salk vaccine developed?   **Polio**

5. Kelts, alevins and grilse are all forms of what?
Salmon

6. What is produced by placing a fodder crop in an airtight structure and letting it ferment? **Silage (Ensilage)**

7. What sort of writings would you associate with Raphael Holinshed? **History**

8. Which English bowler took 9 wickets in an innings against South Africa in 1994? **Devon Malcolm**

9. Which country had a parliament called the Duma? **Russia**

10. What was a psaltery? Was it a musical instrument, a book of psalms or a medicinal herb? **A musical instrument**

11. In which TV hospital does Charlie Fairhead work? **Holby General**

12. Which Scottish footballer was sent home from the 1978 World Cup for taking drugs? **Willie Johnstone**

13. In pickles, what are gherkins? **Cucumbers**

14. Which country is Mexico's largest southern border neighbour? **Guatemala**

15. Who wrote *A Handful of Dust*, *Vile Bodies* and *Decline and Fall*? **Evelyn Waugh**

16. Which of these is not a London Men's Club: Boodles, Forum, Carlton? **Forum**

17. Which Briton was World Motor Racing Champion in 1962 and 1968? **Graham Hill**

18. In which film was Dustin Hoffman 121 years old? ***Little Big Man***

19. In Japan, what is No?   **A type of theatre**

20. In which year was Lady Jane Grey queen?   **1553**

Round 93

1.   Which country's Prime Minister was apparently
     drowned in 1967?   **Australia's**

2.   Where did the Allies first cross the Rhine in World
     War 2?   **Remagen**

3.   Which creature gets its name from the Spanish for
     lizard?   **Alligator**

4.   What is the principal female singer in an opera
     called?   **Prima Donna**

5.   Apart from a toothbrush, what else did the
     audience bring along in *Don't Forget Your
     Toothbrush*?   **Passport**

6.   How many players are there in a hurling team?   **15**

7.   Who was the incurable optimist in *David
     Copperfield*?   **Mr Micawber**

8.   In which field of science would you encounter the
     Pons Asinorum?   **Geometry**

9.   Which meat was used in a Woolton pie?   **None**

10. In which Gilbert and Sullivan operetta does Pooh
     Bah appear?   ***The Mikado***

11. According to the Talmud, what did God do with
     seven handfuls of earth brought to him by the angel
     Azrael?   **He made Adam**

12. Which Duke's seat is Badminton?   **Duke of Beaufort**

13. Which beaten boxer said to his wife in 1926: "Honey, I forgot to duck."?   **Jack Dempsey**

14. Which White House room is the President's office?   **Oval Room**

15. Who played Dr Watson to Basil Rathbone's Sherlock Holmes?   **Nigel Bruce**

16. Which country built the Mannerheim Line as a defence against Russia?   **Finland**

17. Which doctor's suicide note in 1963 said: "I am sorry to disappoint the vultures."?   **Stephen Ward's**

18. Who wrote the novel *Kipps*?   **H G Wells**

19. Which drink's advertising slogan was "It's the real thing."?   **Coca Cola's**

20. Which US general was granted an honorary knighthood by the Queen in 1991?   **Norman Schwarzkopf**

Round 94

1. On the Skull and Crossbones flag, what kind of bones are the crossbones?   **Femurs**

2. Who wrote *Samson Agonistes*?   **John Milton**

3. Who slew the monster Grendel in an old poem?   **Beowulf**

4. If one, two and three are Cardinal, what are first, second and third?   **Ordinal**

5.   Which flower is sometimes called the Lent Lily?
Daffodil

6.   The colour of what in China indicated a mandarin's rank?   **The button on his hat**

7.   Who had 1980s Top Ten Hits with *System Addict*, *Find the Time*, and *Rain or Shine*?   **Five Star**

8.   In the 1960s, which London street was the fashion centre for the young?   **Carnaby Street**

9.   What did you do if you took the King's shilling?
Joined the army

10.   Who interpreted the writing on the wall?   **Daniel**

11.   To what did the expression "lock, stock and barrel" originally refer?   **A gun**

12.   Who in 1993 became the highest scoring Test batsman of all time?   **Alan Border**

13.   Was Angel Beast an old card game, a foodstuff or a cosmetic?   **A card game**

14.   For what is the Athenian, Draco, remembered?
Harsh laws

15.   During which war was the New Model Army formed?   **English Civil War**

16.   Who played the black film detective Shaft?
Richard Roundtree

17.   Who wrote the novel *The Card*?   **Arnold Bennett**

18.   Who said: "The lion and the calf shall lie down together, but the calf won't get much sleep."?
Woody Allen

19. Who was the first US President to be awarded the
     Nobel Peace Prize in 1906?   **Theodore Roosevelt**

20. In a famous children's book what was Cedric
     Errol's title?   **Lord Fauntleroy**

Round 95

1. Which game bird season runs from October 1st to
    February 1st?   **Pheasant**

2. In the art medium tempera, what is mixed with
    powdered paint?   **Egg yolk**

3. What connects these books: *Mein Kampf*, *Pilgrim's
    Progress* and *History of the World*?   **All (partly)
    written in prison**

4. Which was the first American city to host the
    Olympics (1904)?   **St Louis**

5. In which Shakepeare play do Beatrice and Benedick
    appear?   ***Much Ado About Nothing***

6. What did General Wade construct in the Highlands
    from 1724 to 1730?   **Roads**

7. What was the original ominous name for the
    Driver's Safety Device on electric and diesel trains?
                                   Dead Man's Handle

8. To where in Berkshire did CND march from
    London annually for many years?   **Aldermaston**

9. Where did the Germans defeat the Russians over
    the 26th to 30th August in 1914?   **Tannenburg**

10. In which city did the Phoenix Park murders occur in
    1882?   **Dublin**

11. Chelsea, Bow and Spode are all types of what?
     Porcelain

12. Whom did Betty Boothroyd succeed as Speaker of
     the House?   **Bernard Weatherill**

13. Who connects the archaeological programme *Time
     Team* with the comedy series *Blackadder*?   **Tony
     Robinson**

14. Which king hid in an oak tree after the battle of
     Worcester?   **Charles II**

15. What is the occupation of a leprechaun?   **Cobbler**

16. Who wrote *Frenchman's Creek* and *My Cousin
     Rachel*?   **Daphne du Maurier**

17. Who played Lex Luthor in the *Superman* films of
     the 1970s and 1980s?   **Gene Hackman**

18. What was Capability Brown's Christian name?
     Lancelot

19. Where exactly in London were Frost Fairs held
     until 1831?   **On the Thames**

20. Which character's chief opponent was Carl
     Peterson?   **Bulldog Drummond's**

Round 96

1.   Which car manufacturer designed Chris
     Boardman's gold medal-winning bike?   **Lotus**

2.   In *The Screwtape Letters*, who was Screwtape?   **A
     devil**

3. In which play does Gwendolyn Fairfax love Jack Worthing, who was found in a handbag as a baby?
    The Importance of Being Earnest

4. What was the name of the Indian custom in which widows flung themselves on their husbands' funeral pyres?   **Suttee**

5. Which European king died in 1993?   **King Baudouin (Belgium)**

6. Which controversial writer wrote *Time For a Tiger* and *The Kingdom of the Wicked*?   **Anthony Burgess**

7. Which pop group had albums called *Nevermind* and *Bleach*?   **Nirvana**

8. Which British skater won Olympic, European and World titles in 1976?   **John Curry**

9. What was unusual about Derek Jarman's film *Sebastiane*?   **The dialogue was in Latin**

10. Who said: "The bowler's Holding, the batsman's Willey."?   **Brian Johnston**

11. Of which country was Kim Il Sung Prime Minister and President for 46 years?   **North Korea**

12. Which theory of combustion did Antoine Lavoisier demolish in the late 18th century?   **Phlogiston Theory**

13. Who played the TV detective *Banacek*?   **George Peppard**

14. Which fashion designer designs under the Emporio label?   **Armani**

15. Which disease is a virus infection and swelling of the parotid salivary glands?   **Mumps**

16. Which English county's emblem is an imp?
                                    Lincolnshire

17. In Norse mythology, who rode a horse called
     Sleipnir?   **Odin**

18. What is the capital of Pakistan?   **Islamabad**

19. What would you do with a tulwar? Would you
     cook on it, fight with it or keep maps in it?   **Fight**
                                    (It's a sword.)

20. What name was given to the 4th Arab-Israeli War
     of 1973?   **Yom Kippur War**

Round 97

1.   Who would a jerquer work for? A textile factory,
     Customs and Excise or a riding academy?
                            Customs and Excise

2.   Which duo's theatrical performances were called *At
     the Drop of a Hat*?   **Flanders & Swann**

3.   Who played the title role in the film *Shirley
     Valentine*?   **Pauline Collins**

4.   Which part of the body is affected by otitis?   **The ear**

5.   Which country singer and yodeller had a 1955 No 1
     with *Rose Marie*?   **Slim Whitman**

6.   In which country are the Tagalog a major ethnic
     group?   **Philippines**

7.   What was odd about the teenage gang in the film
     The Lost Boys?   **They were vampires**

8.   Which of these countries does NOT drive on the left: New Zealand, Cyprus, Sweden or South Africa?   **Sweden**

9.   What name is given to a pillar or supporting column in the shape of a woman?   **Caryatid**

10. Inguri, Nurek and Guavio are among the world's highest what?   **Dams**

11. In which film did Harrison Ford come from the future to destroy android Rutger Hauer?   ***Blade Runner***

12. Which singing voice is between tenor and soprano?   **Alto**

13. In which country did the lambada dance originate?   **Brazil**

14. Which twentieth century artist has been called The King of Schlock Art?   **Morris Katz**

15. Which series of UK satellites were launched by the USA from 1962 to 1979?   **Ariel**

16. Fullerenes, discovered in 1985, were a new form of which element?   **Carbon**

17. Which European Prime Minister was assassinated in February 1986?   **Olaf Palme**

18. What is measured on the pH scale?
                                            Acidity/Alkalinity

19. What is the traditional dessert on Thanksgiving Day?   **Pumpkin Pie**

20. What are caught in a kheda?   **Elephants**

Round 98

1. Who said of Linford Christie: "He's a well balanced athlete. He's got a chip on each shoulder.'"?   **Derek Redmond**

2. Who won the Tour de France for the third successive time in 1993?   **Miguel Indurain**

3. Complete this literary quartet: Henry, Douglas, Ginger and . . . . . .   **(Just) William**

4. Who played Nora Charles in the *Thin Man* films?   **Myrna Loy**

5. Who recorded albums called *Pandemonium Shadow Show* and *Pussy Cats*?   **Nilsson**

6. Which former US First Lady worked as an editor for the publishers Viking and Doubleday?   **Jackie Onassis**

7. Which fashion designer created the Space Age Collection in 1964?   **Pierre Cardin**

8. Which drug is obtained from the Yellow Cinchona plant?   **Quinine**

9. With what is the organisation CERN concerned?   **Nuclear Research**

10. With which country do you associate tennis player Petr Korda?   **The Czech Republic**

11. What do the Greeks call the Elgin Marbles?   **Parthenon Marbles**

12. How many permanent members are there in the UN Security Council?   **Five**

13. In which country is the TV News Agency Visnews based? **England**

14. In which African country do the Ashanti live? **Ghana**

15. Greek – men; Dutch – maand; German – monat; English – . . . . . (what)? **Month**

16. Which 1912 hoax regarding man's ancestry was not exposed until 1953? **Piltdown Man**

17. Which Oliver Stone war film won Best Picture Oscar in 1986? *Platoon*

18. Which is the longest Classic race? **St Leger**

19. Which pop group's road manager was shot dead in 1986 in Northern Ireland? **Bananarama's**

20. What name is given to the cultivation of plants without soil? **Hydroponics**

Round 99

1. Name the host city of the 2000 AD Olympics. **Sydney**

2. Who was President of Nicaragua from 1981 to 1990? **Daniel Ortega**

3. Who was the first Conservative Prime Minister? **Robert Peel**

4. Which religion has the Kathina festival as a National Holiday? **Buddhism**

5. When it's 12 noon (GMT) in London, what time is it in Casablanca? **12 noon**

6.   What is measured in Criths?   **(Mass of) Gases**

7.   Which country has the Leone as its unit of
currency?   **Sierra Leone**

8.   What was the occupation during the French
revolution of a tricoteuse?   **Knitting**

9.   For what does the abbreviation SJ stand?   **Society
of Jesus**

10.   Who composed the opera *The Bartered Bride*?   **Smetana**

11.   Kislev, Teveth, Sivan and Av are all what?   **Months in the Jewish Calendar**

12.   How many decibels is the noise of busy traffic?   **65 – 70**

13.   Who won the Booker Prize for *The Old Devils*?   **Kingsley Amis**

14.   Who directed *The Quiet Man*, *Rio Grande* and
Stagecoach?   **John Ford**

15.   With which sport would you associate Joe
Montana?   **American Football**

16.   Who would use a Jacquard? An underwater
explorer, a weaver or a gymnast?   **Weaver**

17.   Which painter gave his name to a shade of red?   **Titian**

18.   What does the musical expression 'con fuoco'
mean?   **With fire**

19.   The original King Kong met his fate on the Empire
       State Building. On which landmark did The Amazing
       Colossal Man come to grief?   **Boulder (Hoover)**
                                                      Dam

20.   Whose first solo No 1 was *I'm Still Waiting*?
                                                Diana Ross

Round 100

1.   In which newspaper did the strip cartoon *Jane*
      appear?   *The Daily Mirror*

2.   In which British city is Usher Hall?   **Edinburgh**

3.   On which farm did Worzel Gummidge live?
                                              Scatterbrook

4.   Which fictitious country was ruled by the
      Elphbergs?   **Ruritania**

5.   Who was the first man to drive at more than
      400 mph?   **John Cobb**

6.   Who played the title role in *Young Winston*?
                                               Simon Ward

7.   Who is the patron saint of messengers?   **St Gabriel**

8.   Who recorded albums called *Hounds of Love*, *Never
      For Ever* and *The Whole Story*?   **Kate Bush**

9.   After a gap of many years a new *Carry On* film was
      made in 1992. What was it called?   *Carry On*
                                                 Columbus

10.   Who wrote *Ode To the West Wind*?   **Shelley**

11.   Who turned Ulysses' men into swine?   **Circe**

12. When Wolfe took Quebec, which general did he defeat? **Montcalm**

13. Which horse won the 1993 Grand National? **There was no winner!**

14. Where does a breast buffer work? **In a shoe factory**

15. Which film was made from the book *The Small Woman*? ***The Inn of the Sixth Happiness***

16. If you ordered 'caneton' in a French restaurant what would you get? **Duck**

17. Which country was ruled by William the Lion? **Scotland**

18. Who played Dr Owen in the TV series *Owen MD*? **Nigel Stock**

19. What name is given to the period between Napoleon's escape from Elba to his defeat at Waterloo? **The Hundred Days**

20. In which classic novel did Inspector Javert hunt down Jean Valjean? ***Les Misérables***

THEMATIC QUIZZES

I've always enjoyed both setting and taking part in quizzes that have a theme. If the answers have a theme, the contestants may not know if they have the *right* answers, but they will certainly know if their answers are incorrect.

For instance, if the question master has said that all the answers contain the word 'cat' and then asks: "Who played the negro cook in the film *The Shining*?" the contestants will know that answers such as Godfrey Cambridge, Bernie Casey, Lou Gosset, James Earl Jones and Gregory Hines would all be wrong as none of them contains the word 'cat'. With persistence, the answer 'Scatman Crothers' could then be found.

Similarly, if the theme is that every answer contains a double S, and you are asked "Who was known as The Empress of the Blues?" then obviously answers like Ma Rainey, Ethel Waters and Billie Holiday will not fit the theme, but Bessie Smith would.

Themes are endless. I've taken part in quizzes and set quizzes where there are several rounds and every round has a different theme. Sometimes the theme can run through all the questions, but this makes the evening a little harder for the participants.

Here are a selection of thematic quizzes, but I feel sure that you will enjoy compiling your own.

Good Enough To Eat

All the answers contain something which you can eat.

1. Name the historic region in Europe, partly in Belgium, France and Holland, which was the scene of heavy fighting in both World Wars.   **Flanders**

2. Which religious prisoner wrote his autobiography, *Grace Abounding*, and also began the allegory about Christian's journey to the Celestial City while in prison?   **John Bunyan**

3. What was the former name of Hawaii?   **Sandwich Islands**

4. Which puppet was presented on TV by Annette Mills?   **Muffin the Mule**

5. What is the name of the professor in *Cluedo*?   **Plum**

6. In Greek mythology, what was the name of the place of punishment and perpetual torment in the underworld?   **Tartarus**

7. From which song do these words come: "The sweet things in life to you were just loaned, So how can you lose what you've never owned?"?   ***Life is Just a Bowl of Cherries***

8. Which writer created the lost world of Pellucidar, the lost city of Opar, John Carter, Warlord of Mars and Carson of Venus?   **Edgar Rice Burroughs**

9. What name is given to a sculptured or pictorial representation of the Virgin and the dead Christ?   **Pietà**

10. George Bernard Shaw's play, *Arms and the Man*, was made into which operetta in 1894?   ***The Chocolate Soldier***

11. Which screen character made the following speech? "Italy for 30 years under the Borgias had warfare, terror, murder, bloodshed – they produced Michelangelo, Leonardo Da Vinci and the Renaissance. Switzerland had brotherly love, 500 years of democracy and peace, and what did they produce? The cuckoo clock."   **Harry Lime**

12. Which Israeli group won the Eurovision Song Contest in 1979?   **Milk and Honey**

13. Who, on TV, played Jack Ford in *When the Boat Comes In* and a teacher in *The Beiderbecke Affair*?   **James Bolam**

14. Who is recognised to have been the first man to reach the North Pole?   **Robert Peary**

15. From which poem do the following lines come? "I heard a sound as of scraping tripe / And putting apples wondrous ripe / Into a cider-press's gripe / So munch on, crunch on, take your nuncheon / Breakfast, supper, dinner, luncheon!"   ***The Pied Piper of Hamelin***

16. What code name was given in World War 2 to the prefabricated parts that could be towed across the Channel to construct breakwaters and quaysides where supplies could be unloaded after the D-Day landings?   **Mulberry**

17. What is the eleventh letter of the Greek alphabet?   **Lambda**

18. Which John Steinbeck novel deals with the Joad family, who leave the Oklahoma Dust Bowl in the Depression and head for California?   ***The Grapes of Wrath***

19. In which street did the Fire of London originate?
     Pudding Lane

20. He was an English monk, scholar and scientist who died in 1292. He was nicknamed Doctor Mirabilis. He prophesied aeroplanes, steam engines and telescopes and is credited with having invented gunpowder and the magnifying glass. Who was he?
     Roger Bacon

21. Which dessert was named after the Australian soprano Helen Porter Mitchell?   **Peach Melba**

22. What name is given to the deep limestone shafts in North Yorkshire about four miles from Hawes and about 30 yards from the road? They give their name to the pass between Wensleydale and Swaledale.
     Buttertubs

23. Which American film producer produced the early Bond films as well as such films as *Cockleshell Heroes* and *Chitty Chitty Bang Bang*?   **Cubby Broccoli**

24. He was born Ferdinand Joseph La Menthe and began his career playing piano in brothels in New Orleans. He began recording in the 1920s with his group The Hot Peppers and always claimed that he invented jazz. By what name is he better known?
     Jelly Roll Morton

25. H Allen Smith wrote a satirical novel in which a cat inherited a baseball team. This was made into a film in 1951 with Ray Milland. What was the cat's name?   **Rhubarb**

26. What is the stage name of entertainer Robert Davies?   **Jasper Carrot**

27. Which Yorkshire bowler took 5 for 51 on his Test debut against Pakistan in 1954?   **Bob Appleyard**

28. What was the name of David Copperfield's old nurse?   **Peggotty**

29. What name is given to the flat piece of iron that connects railway rails?   **Fishplate**

30. Of which dance is the following a description? "A ballroom dance popular in the early 1900s, originally performed by black slaves satirizing the elegance of plantation society. Couples walked round in a square and were judged for the grace and inventiveness of their movements."   **Cakewalk**

31. Who had a No 1 hit in 1968 with *Ob-La-Di Ob-La-Da*?   **Marmalade**

32. In which war film did John Wayne stem a Japanese advance by driving a bulldozer into a fuel tank and blowing up himself and the Japanese troops?   ***The Fighting Seabees***

33. Which dynasty has been the ruling dynasty of the Netherlands since 1815?   **Orange**

34. Which Briton was World Motor Racing Champion in 1969, 1971 and 1973?   **Jackie Stewart**

35. Charles, the 2nd Viscount Townshend, brother-in-law of Robert Walpole, was given which nickname because of his interest in certain areas of farming?

Turnip

Double S

All the answers contain SS.

1. In which area did Thomas Hardy set his novels?

Wessex

2. What was the title of the first No 1 by The Police?

Message in a Bottle

3. Lime-flint, Lead-flint, Bohemian and Jena are all kinds of what?

Glass

4. In 1944 Allied forces advancing on Rome were held up by German defensive positions centred on a hill on which was a Benedictine monastery. What was the hill called?

Monte Cassino

5. Of which famous novel is this a summary? The story follows the fortunes of Tom and Maggie Tulliver. Maggie is turned out of the house by Tom, but they become reconciled just before they are both drowned.

The Mill on the Floss

6. Which foreign king married and divorced an Englishwoman named Toni Gardiner?

King Hussein of Jordan

7. Which British film director, with a reputation for being outrageous, made films about Delius, Mahler, Tchaikovsky, Elgar and Debussy?

Ken Russell

8. Which word, which we normally think of as simply meaning a strong emotion, also means the sufferings of Christ on the Cross?   **Passion**

9. Which book contains the service of the mass for the whole year?   **A Missal**

10. What is the capital of the Bahamas?   **Nassau**

11. Which one word means a timber or iron support, to tie up securely and a bundle of hay or straw?   **Truss**

12. Which Roman road ran from Exeter to Lincoln?   **Fosse Way**

13. Which picturesque glen in central Scotland, between Loch Katrine and Loch Achray, was popularised by Sir Walter Scott?   **The Trossachs**

14. Which Frenchman supervised the construction of the Suez Canal?   **Ferdinand de Lesseps**

15. Who was Master of the Queen's Music from 1953 until 1975?   **Sir Arthur Bliss**

16. Which popular garden plant, of which there are about 150 species, comes in varieties such as maritimum and saxatile and has white, pink or yellow flowers?   **Alyssum**

17. Who composed *Songs and Dances of Death*, *A Night on the Bare Mountain* and the opera *Boris Godunov*?   **Mussorgski**

18. Which 20th century novel (made into an acclaimed film in 1984) concerns the friendship of a teacher called Fielding and a doctor called Aziz?   *A Passage To India*

19. Which process, invented in 1855, converts pig iron to steel?   **Bessemer process**

20. Which British pianist initiated lunchtime concerts at the National Gallery during World War 2?

Dame Myra Hess

Birds

All the answers contain a bird.

1. The Bummalo fish, salted and dried, is eaten as a relish called what?   **Bombay Duck**

2. What do we call Rossini's opera *La Gazza Ladra*?

The Thieving Magpie

3. In the USA what name is given to an advanced medical student or recent medical graduate residing in a hospital?   **Intern**

4. Which architect rebuilt 51 London churches after the Great Fire of 1666?   **Christopher Wren**

5. Which is the narrowest part of the English Channel?   **Straits of Dover**

6. What was the title of Arthur Ransome's famous children's book, published in 1931?   ***Swallows and Amazons***

7. What is the nickname of Sheffield Wednesday AFC?   **Owls**

8. What was Manfred Mann's No 1 hit of April 1966?

Pretty Flamingo

9. Which islands in the Atlantic Ocean were named after dogs?   **Canary Islands**

10. Who was the famous wizard who assisted Arthur in the Arthurian legends?   **Merlin**

11. What word describes completing a hole in golf three strokes below par?   **Albatross**

12. For his role in which 1962 film about racial prejudice did Gregory Peck win an Oscar for his portrayal of a small-town lawyer?   ***To Kill a Mockingbird***

13. In a famous song, who was the deadly rival of Ivan Skavinsky Skavar?   **Abdul Abulbul Amir**

14. Which footballer did Alf Ramsey describe as being ten years ahead of his time?   **Martin Peters**

15. Which VTOL fighter was nicknamed The Jump Jet?   **Harrier**

16. Which fruit's other name is the Chinese Gooseberry?   **Kiwi fruit**

17. What was the name of the character played by Dirk Bogarde in the *Doctor* films?   **Simon Sparrow**

18. What name was given to the chalice used by Christ at the Last Supper and later given to Joseph of Arimathea?   **Holy Grail**

19. What was the original name of Drake's ship The *Golden Hind*?   **The *Pelican***

20. Which toy, long popular in China, has now acquired more popularity in the west, especially in the 'stunt' version?   **Kite**

Pen and Ink

All the answers contain either PEN or INK.

1. Who was the first man to win the World Professional
    Snooker Title at the Crucible Theatre in Sheffield?
    John Spencer

2. Who was the Scots born man who founded a
    National Detective Agency in the USA in 1850?
    Allan Pinkerton

3. In Monopoly, which property completes the group
    containing The Angel, Islington, and Euston Road?
    Pentonville Road

4. In which film did Danny Kaye play jazz trumpeter
    Red Nicholls? *The Five Pennies*

5. What is the common name for the fungus called
    Phallus impudicus? **Stinkhorn**

6. Who designed Coventry Cathedral and Sussex
    University? **Basil Spence**

7. Who played The Fonz in TV's *Happy Days*?
    Henry Winkler

8. In *The Hound of the Baskervilles* what was the name
    of the bog into which it was believed the villain
    finally disappeared? **Grimpen Mire**

9. Which song by Adge Cutler and the Wurzels was
    adopted by Bristol City Football Club as their
    theme song? *Drink Up Thy Zider*

10. Which word means 'salary', particularly that paid
    to a clergyman? **Stipend**

11. Which of Mr Pickwick's friends married Arabella
     Allen?   **Nathaniel Winkle**

12. Which carnivorous animal, bred in captivity for its
     fur, has over the years escaped and can now be
     found wild in Britain?   **Mink**

13. Which extremely common object derives its name
     from the Latin for 'a little tail'?   **Pencil**

14. What is the missing word in the following
     quotation? "Joy shall be in heaven over one sinner
     that . . . . ., more than over ninety and nine just
     persons."   **Repenteth**

15. Who ran through the town, upstairs and
     downstairs, in his nightgown?   **Wee Willie Winkie**

16. What term was applied to plays after World War 2
     in which aspects of household life were presented
     fairly realistically?   **Kitchen-sink dramas**

17. What was the name of Dennis Potter's BBC serial in
     which Bob Hoskins played a sheet music salesman
     and actors mimed to 1930s recordings?   *Pennies*
                                            From Heaven

18. Which battle of the Crimean War was fought on
     November 5th, 1854?   **Inkerman**

19. In which event did Mary Peters win an Olympic
     gold medal?   **Pentathlon**

20. What name did Frank Muir give to Joan Bakewell?
                             The Thinking Man's Crumpet

21. On TV, who played the aristocratic Audrey
     Forbes-Hamilton?   **Penelope Keith**

22. Which song from *Sweet Charity* has since become
     strongly associated with Shirley Bassey?   ***Big
                                                      Spender***

23. Who married Belle Elmore, killed her and ran away
     with Ethel Le Neve, the pair of them posing as Mr
     and Master Robinson, but was caught and
     executed?   **Dr Crippen**

24. Where would you see the statue of *The Little
     Mermaid*?   **Copenhagen**

25. What is the translation of Descartes' famous
     statement: "Cogito, ergo sum."?   **I think, therefore
                                                      I am**

26. What do we call a small personal ornament of no
     great value?   **Trinket**

27. Who was the faithful wife of Ulysses?   **Penelope**

28. What was the name of Beatrix Potter's hedgehog
     laundress?   **Mrs Tiggy Winkle**

29. Who said this of exams and examiners: "I should
     have liked to be asked to say what I knew. They
     always tried to ask what I did not know."?
                                   Winston Spencer Churchill

30. Which firm's security warehouse at Heathrow
     Airport was robbed of £26 million worth of gold in
     November 1983?   **Brinks-Mat**

31. Who had Top Ten hits with *Goodbye To Love*, *Top
     of the World* and *Only Yesterday*?   **The Carpenters**

32. In which Ealing film did Googie Withers play a
     publican's wife and Gordon Jackson play the
     chemist's son who falls for her?   ***Pink String and
                                                 Sealing Wax***

33. Which French boxer was World Light Heavyweight Champion from 1920 to 1922 and later fought Jack Dempsey for the World Heavyweight Title?
Georges Carpentier

34. The sculptor, Rodin, was working on a commission when he died. One of the figures from this has become one of his most famous works. What is it called? *The Thinker*

35. What name is often given to a golf course next to the sea? **Links**

36. In which range of Scottish hills is Scald Law the highest peak? **Pentland Hills**

37. Complete this quotation: " Save where the beetle wheels his droning flight / And drowsy . . . . lull the distant fold." **Tinklings**

38. In which film did Kenneth More search for a German battleship? *Sink the Bismarck*

39. Whose first Top Ten hit in 1967 was *See Emily Play*? **Pink Floyd**

40. In which TV series did Jimmy Nail play a Geordie detective? *Spender*

A Christmas Quiz

Round 1
(All the answers have a Christmas connection.)

1. In the theatrical world, what name is given to the financial backer of a stage production? **Angel**

2. Who presents the TV quiz show *Telly Addicts*?
Noel Edmonds

3.   In Cockney Rhyming Slang, what are the 'eyes' called? **Mince Pies**

4.   In which modern country is the site of the ancient city of Troy? **Turkey**

5.   What was the nickname of the historian, Thomas Carlyle? You have a choice of The Star of Bond Street, The Shepherd of Islington or The Sage of Chelsea. **The Sage of Chelsea**

6.   In which TV series did Shirley Jones play David Cassidy's mother before becoming his real step mother? ***The Partridge Family***

7.   Which actress was the first one to travel with Dr Who? **Carol Ann Ford**

8.   By what name is the song *Adeste Fideles* better known? ***O Come, All Ye Faithful***

9.   Was Mickey Rooney born Charles Tinsel, Joe Yule or Frederick Tree? **Joe Yule**

10. Which song contains these lines: "The Rising of the sun, and the running of the deer, the playing of the merry organ"? ***The Holly and the Ivy***

11. What is the common name for the plant *Helleborus Niger*? Is it Christmas Rose, Christmas Lily or Christmas Cactus? **Christmas Rose**

12. Which form of entertainment sprang out of the old Commedia dell'arte, whose central characters were Harlequin and Columbine? **Pantomime**

13. In which TV series does Robbie Coltrane play a psychologist called Fitz? ***Cracker***

14. Which character is played by Richard Attenborough in the 1994 film *Miracle on 34th Street*? **Santa Claus**

15. What did Jack Horner eat in the corner? **Christmas Pie**

16. Which parasitic plant was sacred to the Druids? **Mistletoe**

17. Who was Minister for Education and Science from 1981 to 1986? **Keith Joseph**

18. In which story does Bob Cratchit have a crippled son called Tiny Tim? ***A Christmas Carol***

19. What is the title of Chesterton's poem from which the following lines come? "With monstrous head and sickening cry and ears like errant wings." ***The Donkey***

20. Proverbially, what kind of dog is a person who doesn't want something he has, but won't let anybody else have it? **Dog in a Manger**

Round 2

(All the questions have a Christmas connection.)

1. Which group was at No 1 at Christmas 1974 with *Lonely This Christmas*? **Mud**

2. Of which country is Christmas Island a territory? **Australia**

3. Name one of the two of Santa's reindeer missing from the following list: Dasher, Dancer, Donner, Blitzen, Vixen and Prancer? **Comet or Cupid**

4.   In which year did Santa Claus win the Derby? Was it 1961, 1964 or 1967?   **1964**

5.   Who first recorded the song *Rudolph the Red-Nosed Reindeer* back in 1949?   **Gene Autry**

6.   Who paid £3000 for a turkey in December 1995?   **Linda McCartney**

7.   Who composed the *Christmas Oratorio* in 1734? Was it Bach, Mozart or Brahms?   **Bach**

8.   Who seized the gold of the Nibelungs before being killed himself?   **Siegfried**

9.   What is myrrh? Is it gum resin, a gemstone or an essence distilled from orchids?   **Gum resin**

10.   Who said: "What shall we do with this bauble? There, take it away."?   **Oliver Cromwell**

11.   Which shop in Regent Street is the largest toy shop in the world?   **Hamley's**

12.   In which lake in Hyde Park do members of a local swimming club traditionally take a Christmas Day dip?   **The Serpentine**

13.   Which song begins with these lines: "Sleigh bells ring: are you listening? Down the lane, snow is glistening."?   ***Winter Wonderland***

14.   On whose feast day did Good King Wenceslas look out?   **St Stephen's**

15.   Which scientist, who produced the Laws of Motion, was born on Christmas Day in 1642?   **Isaac Newton**

16.   Which character was played in *Coronation Street* by Lynne Carol? Was it Minnie Caldwell, Ida Barlow or Martha Longhurst?   **Martha Longhurst**

17. Who were walking backwards for Christmas in
    1956?   **The Goons**

18. In which classic film was Holly Martins the central
    character?   *The Third Man*

19. Which British territory surrendered to the Japanese
    on Christmas Day in 1941? Was it Singapore, Hong
    Kong or Sarawak?   **Hong Kong**

20. In Raymond Briggs' story *The Snowman*, what's the
    name of the little boy whom the snowman takes to
    Santa Claus's party? Is it Robert, James or
    Andrew?   **James**

And a Christmas Quiz Tie Breaker:

In which year was the first pantomime produced in
Britain?   **1717**

TIE BREAKER QUESTIONS

1. In what year did Gregory I become Pope? **590**

2. How many symphonies did Haydn compose? **104**

3. How long, in miles, is the River Clyde? **106**

4. In what year did Apache chief Cochise die? **1876**

5. When was W G Grace born? **1848**

6. When did Henry VIII meet Francis I on the Field of the Cloth of Gold? **1520**

7. In what year did Sir Arthur Sullivan die? **1900**

8. When was the first photocopier marketed? **1907**

9. In what year was Michelangelo born? **1475**

10. When was Arizona admitted to the Union? **1912**

11. In what year did Britain capture Gibraltar from Spain? **1704**

12. How long, in miles, is the Grand Canyon? **280**

13. When did Stephen become King of England? **1135**

14. When did Saladin capture Jerusalem? **1187**

15. How many species of pigeons and doves are there? **289**

16. How high, in feet, is Nelson's column and statue?
185

17. In what year did Roman Emperor Augustus die?
4 AD

18. When did John Keats die?   **1821**

19. When did Marlborough win the Battle of Malplaquet?   **1709**

20. When did Sir Arthur Conan Doyle die?   **1930**

21. When was Duke Ellington born?   **1899**

22. When was the Northumberland Plate first run?
1833

23. When did Sir Walter Raleigh die?   **1618**

24. When was Pretoria founded?   **1855**

25. When did Siegfried Sassoon die?   **1967**

26. When was the Mogul Empire established?   **1526**

27. When did Canning become British Prime Minister?   **1827**

28. In what year did Nostradamus die?   **1566**

29. In what year was *The Wind in the Willows* first published?   **1908**

30. When were the Royal Marines founded?   **1644**

31. When was the hymn *Onward, Christian Soldiers* written?   **1864**

32. In what year did the Wars of the Roses begin?   **1455**

33. When were people killed by an earthquake in Colchester?   **1884**

34. When was the Panama Canal opened?   **1914**

35. In what year did Britain annex New Zealand?   **1840**

36. What is the area of Zanzibar in square miles?   **641**

37. What is the diameter of the sun in miles?   **864,000**

38. When did Britain have its first Socialist MP?   **1892**

39. In what year did St Bernard's win the Scottish
FA Cup?   **1895**

40. How many dollars did a Model T Ford cost
in 1925?   **290**

41. When did Robert Clive commit suicide?   **1774**

42. When was Sir Walter Scott born?   **1771**

43. When was Jesse James killed?   **1882**

44. When did Harvey discover the circulation
of the blood?   **1780**

45. When was Sigmund Freud born?   **1856**

46. When did Amelia Bloomer invent bloomers?   **1850**

47. When was Al Capone born?   **1899**

48. When did Flamsteed become the first
Astronomer Royal?   **1675**

49. When was the Royal Geographical Society
founded?   **1830**

50. When was the rotary printing press invented?   **1844**

51. What was the 1994 population of Zurich?   **422,000**

52. When did Luther nail his 95 theses to the
Wittenburg church door?   **1517**

53. When was the SPCK founded? **1698**

54. When was the OBE introduced? **1917**

55. When was a Second Division added to the Scottish Football league? **1893**

56. When was Rugby School founded? **1567**

57. When was Nat King Cole born? **1919**

58. When was the first part of the Oxford English Dictionary published? **1884**

59. When did the first school magazine appear? **1774**

60. When did Peter the Great become Czar of Russia? **1547**

61. What was Jackie Howard's world record for sheep sheared in a single day? **321**

62. In what year was London Zoo established? **1826**

63. When did Tennyson become Poet Laureate? **1850**

64. When was the National Trust founded? **1895**

65. When did the New York subway system begin? **1868**

66. When was the electric flat-iron invented? **1882**

67. How long, in feet, was the *Queen Elizabeth*? **1031**

68. When did Cartwright invent the power loom? **1785**

69. When was the first US trans-continental railway completed? **1869**

70. When was the Atlantic first crossed by steamship? **1826**

71. When was the term 'omnibus' first applied to a public transport vehicle? **1828**

72. When was Henry VIII born? **1491**

73. When did Edward VI die? **1553**

74. When was oil lighting first used on the streets of London? **1681**

75. When did the poet John Milton die? **1674**

76. When did William Pitt the Younger die? **1806**

77. When was the Bank of Scotland founded by the Scottish Parliament? **1695**

78. When were the Quakers founded? **1647**

79. When was Bishop Ridley burned at the stake? **1555**

80. When did the Mutiny on the Bounty take place? **1789**

81. When did Big Ben come into service? **1859**

82. When was the *Daily Mail* newspaper founded? **1896**

83. When did William Hedley invent the locomotive *Puffing Billy*? **1813**

84. When did Thomas Tenison become Archbishop of Canterbury? **1694**

85. When was Joan of Arc burned at the stake? **1431**

86. When was Edinburgh University founded? **1582**

87. When did Edward III burn Aberdeen? **1336**

88. When did Jane Austen die? **1817**

89. When was cockfighting made illegal? **1849**

90. When was Letchworth, the first garden city, founded?   **1903**

91. When was the first performance of *Peter Pan*?   **1904**

92. When was linoleum invented?   **1860**

93. When were the Tolpuddle Martyrs transported?
                                                       1834

94. When was the first British landing on Rockall Island?   **1810**

95. When was Adam Smith's *Wealth of Nations* published?   **1776**

96. When were the Grenadier Guards founded?   **1656**

97. When did Catherine Parr marry Henry VIII?   **1543**

98. When did Scotland finally lose Berwick to England?   **1482**

99. When was Connecticut first settled?   **1635**

100. When was Richard I ransomed and released?   **1194**

RIGHT WAY
PUBLISHING POLICY

HOW WE SELECT TITLES

RIGHT WAY consider carefully every deserving manuscript. Where an author is an authority on his subject but an inexperienced writer, we provide first-class editorial help. The standards we set make sure that every **RIGHT WAY** book is practical, easy to understand, concise, informative and delightful to read. Our specialist artists are skilled at creating simple illustrations which augment the text wherever necessary.

CONSISTENT QUALITY

At every reprint our books are updated where appropriate, giving our authors the opportunity to include new information.

FAST DELIVERY

We sell **RIGHT WAY** books to the best bookshops throughout the world. It may be that your bookseller has run out of stock of a particular title. If so, he can order more from us at any time – we have a fine reputation for "same day" despatch, and we supply any order, however small (even a single copy), to any bookseller who has an account with us. We prefer you to buy from your bookseller, as this reminds him of the strong underlying public demand for **RIGHT WAY** books. Readers who live in remote places, or who are housebound, or whose local bookseller is uncooperative, can order direct from us by post.

FREE

If you would like an up-to-date list of all **RIGHT WAY** titles currently available, please send a stamped self-addressed envelope to

ELLIOT RIGHT WAY BOOKS,
KINGSWOOD, SURREY, KT20 6TD, U.K.

or visit our web site at www.right-way.co.uk